ENCOUNTER WITH NOTHINGNESS

ENCOUNTER WITH NOTHINGNESS

An Essay on Existentialism

by

Helmut Kuhn

Professor of Philosophy at
Emory University

The King's Library

GREENWOOD PRESS, PUBLISHERS
WESTPORT, CONNECTICUT

Library of Congress Cataloging in Publication Data

Kuhn, Helmut, 1899-
    Encounter with nothingness.

    Reprint of the 1949 ed. published by Regnery,
Hinsdale, Ill., which was issued as no. 11 of the
Humanist library.
    1. Existentialism.   I. Title.
B819.K8 1976   142'.7   74-29635
ISBN 0-8371-7982-3

Copyright 1949

HENRY REGNERY COMPANY

Originally published in 1949 by Henry Regnery Company,
Hinsdale, Illinois

Reprinted with the permission of Henry Regnery Company

Reprinted in 1976 by Greenwood Press,
a division of Williamhouse-Regency Inc.

Library of Congress Catalog Card Number 74-29635

ISBN 0-8371-7982-3

Printed in the United States of America

ACKNOWLEDGMENT

I owe the leisure needed for writing this book to a grant-in-aid allocated by the Committee on Research at Emory University, from funds made available jointly by the Carnegie Foundation and Emory University. The author alone, however, is responsible for the statements made in this publication.

H. K.

TABLE OF CONTENTS

CHAPTER   PAGE

Introduction   ix

I. What is Existence?   1

II. Nothingness Astir   9

III. Estrangement   24

IV. Subjective Truth   43

V. Gravediggers at Work   69

VI. Condemned to be Free   84

VII. The Crisis of the Drama   103

VIII. Illumination through Anguish   124

IX. Beyond Crisis   147

TWO ENCOUNTERS:

The Advocate of Passion, tempting
the Soul, speaks:
"Is it nothing — that Nothing which
delivers us from everything?"
> (Paul Claudel, *Le Soulier de Satin*)

God summons His Servant:
"The threshold shook and a cloud filled
the temple. Then I said: 'Woe to me,
I am Nothing."
> (Isaiah 6:5)

Introduction

AN ATTEMPT is made in this book to explain a philosophy which has recently come to be known under the name of Existentialism. I am well aware of the diversity of ideas and tendencies covered by this name. But I also believe that through the diversity a uniform pattern of thought can be discerned. This pattern the following chapters try to unfold, with due regard to the individuality of the writers who will be heard as witnesses. The emphasis is on the principles rather than on the details of execution. No compendium is intended, but rather a compass for the guidance of readers.

I do not agree with those who belittle Existentialism as an ephemeral fashion. I agree even less with others who hold that Existentialism is perhaps relevant for the Old Continent but irrelevant for America. Their regionalism has no place in philosophy. Besides, the facts are against them. When William James countered the claims and quarrels of speculative philosophy with the question: "What difference does it make to us in living our lives?" he struck out in the direction of Existentialism. The American novel is among the influences that have shaped the Existentialist movement in France. An American, Reinhold Niebuhr, is prominent in the Existentialist trend of Protestant theology; the American drama, especially with Eugene O'Neill and Maxwell Anderson, is imbued with Existentialist ideas, and so is the poetry of W. H. Auden. "All deep, earnest thinking is but the intrepid effort of the soul to keep the open independence of her sea; while the wildest winds of heaven and earth conspire to cast her on the treacherous, slavish shore." This premonition of Existentialism's "mortally intolerable truth" is taken from a great American writer, Herman Melville (*Moby Dick*, Chap. 23). To maintain academic aloofness in the face of growing interest on the part of other people does not seem the course of wisdom for American philosophers. I do not imply, however, that the excitement over the novel phenomenon displayed outside the academic fold is all enlightened enthusiasm—far from it. But the deeper the confusion, the more urgent the demand for explanation.

This is not an Existentialist treatise on Existentialism. In part only do I find it possible to agree with the philosophy under analysis. The teachers of this philosophy hold that it is necessary for man to die in order to live. The walls which enclose us, they think, must be broken down in order to open a vista towards our true horizon. Man must be brought to a crisis. In this the Existentialists seem to me in accord with the great teachers of humanity and, in fact, with truth itself. This far I follow them willingly. But I disagree on the question of the nature of that reality which is to shatter the screens and shelters around us. In Existentialism crisis is conceived as an encounter with "Nothingness," that is, the privation of meaning and reality, whereas, in truth, it seems to me that it is the incomprehensible fullness of meaning and reality, God alone, who is the rightful claimant to the role of the saving destroyer. The Existentialists take the road to Calvary. But arriving there they find the place empty except for two thieves dying on their crosses.

I would not find it worth while mentioning this disagreement had it not furnished the point of view from which Existentialism has become intelligible to me. One might object that it would be preferable for an interpreter to forget about his own point of view and to let things speak for themselves. I am too much in agreement with Existentialism to find much meaning in this objection. I am willing to admit that, since sunlight has certain color qualities, the green I see before me is actually green-as-seen-in-sunlight. But I do not think it is reasonable to wait for darkness in order to find out what the real color of foliage might be.

Existentialism is designed to do something to us, to seize upon the whole mind, and in this respect it is more authentically philosophical than much of what is included in our academic curricula under the title of philosophy.

Existentialism as it comes in touch with the living mind arrests its normal processes of thought and will, and then again precipitates them into fresh activity. The rhythm of this action is the rhythm of all life—pause followed by release of energy. But this all-pervasive rhythm is intensified in Existentialist thought to the point of violence. The pause becomes crisis, the fresh beginning a rebirth. In this again, Existentialism is faithful to the law in our minds.

In living our lives we think and will something. This something thought and willed is infinitely complex and rich, and as a rule we do not wonder in what precisely it consists. We prepare for and we practice a profession; we fall in love and we get married; we buy a car and build a house to live in; we hope that a world government will succeed in imposing peace, and we vote for the candidate most likely to promote this end. And in our eagerness to achieve the manifold purposes which grow upon us out of the moving pattern of our lives, we surrender ourselves without being aware of this abandon. Those multiple interests do not confront us—rather, we live in them. We are our interests. To live means for us not to stop, not to take stock of the variety of things thought and willed. Life is attention to objectives upon which we are bent in the almost literal sense of this word, and each one of these objectives is concrete, exacting, and obtrusive even while it fails to be absorbing. Life, in one word, is pursuit.

Life is pursuit—until it is forced to a standstill. Existentialist philosophy undertakes so to arrest us. Through Plato we are accustomed to think of the life of the soul under the image of a charioteer trying to master two unequal steeds. The Existentialist (of whom I now think as a type, the Existentialist in us) pulls the reins sharply back and then, when the horses, brought to a sudden halt, rear on their haunches, he cracks the whip.

Generally in life we are stopped by an obstacle. Some objective proves unattainable. Then we fret and chafe, subsiding finally in bitterness, or, the more frequent course of events, we find consolation in objectives more easily reached. We circumvent the obstacle and continue in pursuit. The Existentialist does not add a new, more formidable obstacle in order to arrest us effectively. Instead of throwing into our path something that might serve as a barrier, he arrests us with—nothing. You are free, he tells us; nothing constrains you. But since this nothing exerts so powerful an action on the mind—it achieves what all the combined powers of nature and man are unable to achieve—since nothing forces upon our reluctant ego the unnatural pause, we may well raise it to the status of a quasi essence and speak of nothingness. The halt imposed by Existentialism is an Encounter with Nothingness.

The Existentialist philosopher asks: what, in thinking and willing, do you ultimately and seriously think and will? What do you think with the assurance of relevant knowledge, disclosed to you as reliable truth concerning yourself and the world in which you live? The answer comes in the form of negations: it is not what science teaches me, for this is patchwork and of uncertain applicability to life. It is not what I think of myself, or of my friends, or my country, for this is surmise, estimate, or at best probable opinion. What do you will with unwavering devotion, so that everything else is willed and loved only for the sake of this first objective and greatest good? Again the reply will be a string of negations: not the promotion of what belongs in the field of my professional duties; not wife, children, and friends; not wealth, learning, or power; not higher living standards for all men; not . . . and in so passing from negation to negation I, as Existentialist, obliterate this rich and complex world in which we sometimes so comfortably live—the world which our thinking and willing builds up for us. As this world, deprived of ultimate meaning and cohesion, crumbles, there rears itself behind it, more real than Being, the origin of all negations, Nothingness. This is the true arrest, the total paralysis. But the experience does not come as abruptly and dramatically as this account may suggest. When the

Existentialist shows the abyss, we are startled. But at
the bottom of our minds we may also feel that we knew
all this before, that we had been standing at the brink of
the abyss all our life and we dared not confess it. We
had preferred to play with our baubles. . . . Now we
look up and ask the unanswerable question: why is there
something rather than Nothing?

The Existentialist claims to initiate us, through acquaintance with Nothingness, into the maturity of disillusionment. This claim faithfully expresses a thought
latent in the deeds and events which compose our contemporary world. To that extent Existentialism is truthful.
In spite of the highly technical language of the book, one
might describe Sartre's *L'être et le néant,* one of the chief
documents of contemporary Existentialism, as "journal-
ism." Nothingness, active futility, is afoot among us here
and now, in the hearts of this our generation. The movement of the *néant néantisant* (the naughting naught) in
Sartre's treatise reflects the actions of peoples and individuals shouting peace and bent on mutual destruction,
proclaiming progress and descending deeper into barba-
rism. In the past—broadly speaking, until 1914—it was
the privilege of prophetic individuals to warn us tha the
times were out of joint. As an obvious though inconclusive
objection to these warnings people derived comfort from
the fact that the market continued to expand, that industry flourished, mortality rates sank, inventions multiplied, that the whole machinery of civilization was still
in working order. It is no longer in order. From a subtle
intimation, Nothingness has grown into a stark reality. A
destructive war against tyranny was fought, and now, after
its victorious termination, an estimated fifteen millions
languish in captivity for political reasons. Meanwhile, the

science of matter furnishes the weapons for the destruction of as much of the material world as is within human reach. So it has been demonstrated to us that even after the presiding purpose and the ultimate devotion have ceased to enlighten and to organize the things thought and willed by man, markets may expand, industries flourish, and food abound—for a while. But this while—the life term granted to a social body whose soul has fled—seems almost exhausted. The machinery itself is on the point of disintegration, and as Nought expands, the Existentialists, birds of ill omen, herald its dominion.

The truth of Existentialism is not limited to that of a cultural symptom. Over and above the timeliness of this philosophy—an ambiguous recommendation for all but the most ephemeral things—it reaffirms a universal truth about man. Man must purchase victory at the price of an ultimate defeat. But the grave question before us is whether Existentialism interprets this law of crisis correctly. This philosophy grants to Nothingness a quasi-substantial reality. Nothingness is to be encountered in despair, to be grasped in the light of anguish until, thanks to the resilience of his self-assertive will, man emerges into the untrammeled freedom of his selfhood. He must become homeless in order to learn about his divinity.

To this Existentialist interpretation of crisis is opposed another teaching. It is suggested that the Nothing on which Existentialists enlarge is actually the Nothingness of our own selves in their remoteness from God. Instead of being the quasi-existing object of anguished apprehension, Nothingness appears only at the margin of Supreme Reality, coperceptible, if I may use this term, rather than perceptible by itself, and yet able to arouse the longing of perverted passion in flight from reality. Anguish, as culti-

vated and analyzed by the Existentialists, is adulterated
with longing for death, the voluptuousness of the spirit.
In the saving crisis, however, fear and anguish are on
the surface only, as the palpitations of a trembling love.

The following pages are chiefly concerned with clarify-
ing this alternative. We are indebted to Existentialism for
pressing upon us the necessity of making up our minds
about the meaning of crisis. No haphazard conclusion but
an intelligent decision is required, everyone being judge
in this matter for himself. This is an important decision.
However small the individual's radius of action, his error
cannot fail to hasten the downfall in which we are
involved, just as the right choice will infallibly count
towards redemption.

The history of thought since the decline of philosophical
idealism during the earlier part of the nineteenth century
has been characterized by a succession of minds passionately one-sided rather than richly harmonized, tragically
suffering rather than matured through affliction, keenly
sensitive rather than wise. Those who did not simply play
the game of the time by preaching the Kingdom of Man
as the tool-making animal and salvation through industry
were forced into isolation and, as protesting outsiders and
warners, they spoke with a strident voice to make themselves heard by their complacent century. They purchased
power at the price of balance. Reverence for measure
and norm, the marks of classic achievement, were foreign
to them.

Contemporary Existentialism can be described as a
renaissance of Kierkegaard, one of the titanic sufferers
of the anticlassic age. The emphasis on despair as a sick-

ness unto death, on the unreconciled cleavage of the mind and spiritual death in the anguish of crisis, while peculiar in form to Kierkcgaard, marks him also as a brother to Marx, Carlyle, Tolstoy, Dostoyevsky, and Nietzsche. Regarding this characteristic emphasis, modern Existentialists tend to be more Kierkegaardian than Kierkegaard. For Kierkegaard, the passage through the desert of Nothingness is preliminary to the acquisition of the promised land of faith. For the non-Christians among his modern followers (and they are more distinctively Existentialist than the Christian members of the school), the preamble has become the message itself: they invite us to pitch our tents in the desert and to forget about promised lands.

Faith counteracted by reason, as in Kierkegaard; man rebellious in an estranged society, as in Marx; the heart given the lie by mocking intellect, as in Dostoyevsky; pride unable to come to terms with human finitude, as in Nietzsche—of all these elements of spiritual anxiety the aroma and quintessence is in Existentialism. After a succession of the masters of unbalance—indirect and involuntary witnesses of truth, cross-bearers without faith— there follow in our time the Existentialist doctrinaires of unbalance, providing the formula for anxiety and picking up the nodal point of the previous nihilistic trend. They, at long last, divulge the secret of the frenzy that agitated Marx in penning his indictment of all previous history, that Dostoyevsky put into the hearts of his creatures (saints caricatured into suicides and maniacs or diabolical destroyers), or that fills the hollow grandiloquence of the Sermon on the Superman with resounding pathos. The Existentialists make it clear what was going on in the minds of these their predecessors: there has been traffic with Nothingness. Making a deal with Nothingness, the

Existentialists proclaim, is man's universal lot, and they offer to teach us the rules of this fearful intercourse. As philosopher-historians they tell the story of the Encounter with Nothingness, and as masters of ceremonies they provide for its properly taking place.

Codifiers and systematizers that they are, the Existentialists bring up the rear of the procession of "problematic" thinkers of the nineteenth century. There is nothing inarticulate and inchoate in their writings. Nothingness has long been lurking; they bring it out into the open. Especially Sartre offers nihilism in a nutshell. So much are the Existentialists heirs and late-comers that, in spite of the sensation they succeeded in creating, one may wonder whether their message is not actually a belated one. Kierkegaard, Carlyle, and Nietzsche were solitaries rousing a complacent generation. Is this our era of the great wars still a time to rouse and startle? It seems so, otherwise the success achieved by the Existentialists would be inexplicable. But the moment for rousing calls is fast slipping away, and even now the complacency which is left lacks in confidence and resembles hebetude induced by fear. As the area of facile optimism contracts, a less truncated truth than the one offered by Existentialism will be in order. That superficial antithesis—philosophy of crisis *versus* complacent dogmatic construction—will then be brushed aside to give room to a better insight which the Existentialists herald (the rearguard being a vanguard as well) but which eludes their grasp. Quietives rather than incentives will be in demand, and under the pressure of this situation it may once more become clear that the true catalytic of despair and crisis is the vision of harmony and peace—because this peace is not ours but God's. Crisis as depicted by the Existentialists is the

Christian crisis in caricature. The original is recognizable, just as in Daumier's cartoons representing court procedures the judge is recognizably a judge. But the effigy represents also the opposite of the supposed model.

A correspondence point by point makes the likeness evident: Christian is the idea of crisis itself and of rebirth, of a dread passage through despair and consciousness of guilt; Christian the emphasis placed on the supreme hour of death, on the individual on whose free decision weal and woe depend and who is yet finite, not spirit encased in a body but body-spirit, interpenetration and fusion of the physical and psychical. But each of these features is so twisted within the Existentialist pattern of thought that a terrifying yet meaningful distortion results. The Encounter initiating crisis is not an encounter with God who discovers our Nothingness but with Nothingness as the vacuum left by the nonexistent God as in Sartre, or the absent God as in Heidegger. Rebirth does not issue in the new childhood of faith but in the hardened masculinity of the superman. The consciousness of guilt is not consciousness of sin, that is, of failure to be like unto God, but the separateness of existence itself is viewed as guilt. Freedom is not rational choice guided by pre-existing norms and impeded by both the infirmity of will and the dimness of vision but, for the Existentialist, it is the creation of norms out of nothing. For the Christian, death is a dual reality—for each one the *hora suprema* in the sense of a last chance and a last peril, the moment in which a whole lifetime may be confirmed or annulled, and, at the same time, it is death of the beloved person, in which latter form alone it achieves its final terror and majesty. Whereas, then, the Christian teaching about Christ's atoning death is based upon the duality of the human experience of death, the glance of the Existentialist, especially of Heidegger, is riveted to that single event towards which the life of every one of us moves as to its goal and termination. From this disparity the fundamental disagreement about life results: life is not life temporal in which life eternal germinates, but it is temporality through and through, the Existentialist affirms. With a concordant voice Hellenic philosophy and Christian faith exhort us "to think the deathless." "Think death!" comes the Existentialist's rejoinder.

Modifying Pascal's celebrated words on man's grandeur and misery, we may assert that it is not good to push man into despair in the hope of effecting a healing crisis; nor is it good to give him easy comfort by confirming his high hopes. Simultaneously rather and as in one breath we must speak to him of despair as well as of hope but so that hope is viewed as growing out of despair. Again, this can be done only by making despair specific, concrete and private, bound up with our particular failures, and by making hope universal and sharable by holding out an achievement to which we may aspire and which, at the same time, must be bestowed upon us as a gift. Existentialism reverses this order, making despair universal and hope private. But it profits us nothing to look upon the spectacle of a crumbling civilization as revelatory of Nothingness. We shall rather be called to account for specific failures of which we are guilty collectively or individually. And these specific failures, both commissions and omissions, may then be found to spring from one basic failure—the surrender of hope.

Unbalance is elevated to the rank of a principle by the Existentialist removal of the counterweight which, in Christian thought, prevents crisis from breaking up human nature and which renders a Christian humanism possible. This counterpoising and stabilizing element we call ascent.

Ascent signifies progress in knowledge: from the things easiest to know and to control—the realm of inanimate matter—we rise to the things of which it is harder to know much and which can be controlled in part only or not at all—to living things and man. But this cognitive rise must have a foundation in reality. We could not so scale upward, were not reality itself constructed as an order of tiers, rising from the primitive to the richly organized. Accordingly, reason in whose light we ascend must be conceived of as a power which by its very nature is "hierarchical," that is, disposed in an order of ranks. Finally, ascent, while being essentially a cognitive process, is also more than theory, more than a gradual unveiling of reality. It is a widening and self-disclosure of the whole mind, a rise in the order of attachments, a training of the affective power by which we learn to love things in their proper order, each in the measure of its dignity.

There is no ascent without the summit towards which to ascend—without God—in the order of knowledge, lucidity itself, yet hardest to know for us; in the order of reality, ultimate cause; in the order of affection, the First Love. God is arrived at by the intellect through negations. He is the one that is not known at any level, however exalted, of mundane knowledge, not attained at any level of creaturely perfection. Since He is thus the source of negations we may, adopting the paradoxical language of the mystics, call Him Nought. But He is nought only in the sense of a superabundance which annihilates limitations and distinctions. The impoverishment involved in ascent (we rise to that which is most knowable by itself, but least knowable to us) is merely the obverse side of infinite enrichment. For the negations of ascent are not absolute. The creation as a whole as well as in all its parts is *not* God, and in this far God is the hidden God, the "wholly other." At the same time the created things, in varying degrees of clarity, are a likeness of God. The God to whom we can ascend through infinitely remote analogies is revealed in His creation.

Ascent placed in the center of spiritual life may be ruinous to the mind by fostering the pride of intellect coupled with pride of achievement. For the sake of our integrity ascent, the intellectual pole of inner life, must be kept in balance by the humiliation of crisis in which our practical life centers. Crisis, rightly understood, is the shattering experience of our impotence—a misery out of which we may be lifted but from which we are unable to rise by our own strength. This brings us to the fundamental weakness of Existentialism. In this philosophy crisis is paramount, while ascent is obliterated. The likenesses and analogies of God are erased and negation becomes absolute. The Nothingness which the Existentialist encounters is the shadow of the repudiated God.

I

What is Existence?

WE DISTINGUISH between *what* a thing is and *that* it is. What a thing is we call its essence, that it is, its existence. The thing I hold in my hand is by essence a pencil. And this pencil, as I believe on the evidence of my senses, exists.

As men of theory, we are generally interested in what things are like in their essences, and their existence is taken for granted. We are, as a rule, not excited about the existence of light. We wish rather to know its nature or essence.

Defining the essence is always a difficult, complicated and, in most cases, an unending business. The question of existence, on the other hand, confronts us with a simple alternative. Either a thing exists or it does not exist. There is no third possibility, though there are many doubtful cases.

The question of existence is urged upon us chiefly by our interest. We raise it when we care for the existence or the nonexistence of something. When darkness closes down, we do get excited about the existence of light. God, spies in our midst in time of war, a famine in Europe, a

personal debt—these are objects about whose existence
we worry, and with reference to them the question of
essence, however important, will be regarded as secondary: its solution appears instrumental in settling that
other more insistent problem. So we do not bother about
existence unless existence is called in question. The concern for existence is bound up with concern about possible
nonexistence, and vice versa.

In so explaining the term existence we follow common
usage. Now we note a curious departure from it. Modern
Existentialist philosophy, while continuing to speak of
existence in the ordinary sense, confers upon it also a
narrower and more emphatic meaning. Existence, in this
more specific sense, is ascribed to the human individual
and moreover, in a move towards still greater specificity,
to man as animated by spiritual zeal. So, from a simple
affirmation of "being there," existence becomes partly
a universally human quality (man's particular mode of
"being there"), partly a title of honor. To have true existence, to be an existing individual—this appears as a mark
of distinction granted only to the impassioned and intellectually alert personality.

This is not an arbitrary twisting of the word. The promotion of the term "existence" to unsuspected philosophical honors results from an experience which, though not
novel in itself, is, for the first time, given a central place.
The terminological innovation presupposes and expresses
an Encounter with Nothingness.

The problem of existence, we repeat, generally springs
from concern about existence or nonexistence. I am concerned about the existence of the passport in my pocket,
and this concern implies the idea of its possible nonexistence—I may have lost it. Or I am concerned about the

nonexistence of a contagious disease in our town, and this implies an apprehension as to its possible existence. So, whenever the existence of something is pointed up to us by the interest we take in it, the possible nonexistence of that same thing emerges as a twin phenomenon, as the shadow, so to speak, cast by existence. In observing this shadow we do not encounter nothingness but only the negation of that particular object of our interest. And this interest of ours, vitally concerned as it is with the either-or, being or not-being, gives rise to the questions: Why is this? or, why is this not?

There are degrees of interest, and accordingly the question of existence is more or less burning. At its pole of extreme intensity it is a question of salvation and perdition. Likewise, there is a variety of objects of interest, ranging in magnitude from the penny in my pocket to the universe. The latter object, which embraces all other objects, also casts its negative shadow, and the non-Being of this total object is total non-Being—Nothingness. It is no less natural for man to be concerned about the existence of the world than to worry about the existence of the penny in his pocket. Of course, he cannot reasonably doubt the fact that, in one way or other, the world does exist. But he may reasonably be in doubt as to whether it exists as "world," that is, as an organized, meaningful whole, a creation, rather than as the brute sum total of things blown together by the winds of chance. As this doubt deepens into despair, it gives rise to a negative interest in the existence of all that exists. The desperate and audacious question is asked: Why is there something rather than nothing? This is the expression of the Encounter with Nothingness in the medium of philosophical thought.

The question of existence is bound up with the human

interest in existence and nonexistence. This observation
tempts the Existentialist philosopher into giving the analysis of existence a subjective turn. We take an interest in
the existence of the penny in our pocket or in the nonexistence of the world. But, the Existentialist asks, are
not these manifold and changing interests rooted in one
basic and persistent interest—the interest which man
takes in his own existence? This being so, we are justified
in ascribing existence in a more specific sense to that
being which in existing is infinitely concerned about his
existence. For it is true that the meaning though not the
fact of the difference between existence and nonexistence
of things other than man is derived from, or at any rate
elucidated by, man's passionate interest in his own existence, or his equally passionate fear of annihilation.

This more specific use of the term existence in the sense
of human existence comes very close to restating an
ancient metaphysical truth. Metaphysically considered,
things as existing are animated by a tendency to maintain
themselves in existence. The inertial character of motion
and the biological instinct of self-preservation testify on
different levels to the same principle. On the human level
this cleaving to one's own existence (*suum esse praeservare*)
assumes a transbiological form: it reveals itself as the desire
for salvation, the longing for life eternal.

There is, however, a significant difference between this
metaphysical view and the Existentialist innovation. The
former sees man as encompassed by the brotherly communion of the universe; the latter isolates him by stressing
alone (and thereby overstressing) the uniqueness of the
human concern for existence. Furthermore, according to
the metaphysical view, all beings, including man, are
naturally directed towards preservation or enhancement

of being, although there is for man also a lure away from this ascending path, an evil yearning downwards into obliteration, the fascination of the depths. Conversely, the Existentialist discards the idea of a nature tending towards its own perfection. For him the human concern for existence is a continual wresting of existence from the abyss of nonexistence, a self-assertion in the face of the perpetually imminent threat of spiritual annihilation by a world which is alien to our human aspirations. The encounter with nothingness is no longer viewed as one of the dangers and temptations besetting man (a temptation which, if faced and resisted, can be productive of spiritual growth); it is regarded as the very hub of human life, the initiation to maturity, the preamble to faith.

Existence and its concomitant, nonexistence, or being and non-being, are linked with each other by possibility. The existence of a thing involves the possibility of its nonexistence and again, non-being refers us to possible being. It follows that the negative interest in the totality of existence—the encounter with Nothingness expressed in the query: Why is there something rather than nothing?—tinctures the whole of reality with the hue of mere possibility. Things, of course, continue to exist. But their existence appears as accidental. They happen to be, though they might just as well not be. They are stamped with all-pervasive contingency.

To live and to act means for man: giving existence to the merely possible. So he is not only existing in an emphatic sense of the word (being in his existence infinitely concerned about it)—he is also the source of existence. His life is the transformation into existence of the nonexistent as the possible. It is, in other words, an exercise of freedom. Viewed in the light of the experience of the encounter with Nothingness, human freedom is absolute.

This is not to say that man is free to do what he pleases. Evidently he is not. By the absoluteness of his freedom is meant that the limiting conditions are the indifferent material out of which anything may be made. Within these limits an infinite number of choices can be made. No essence or law of human nature, no predetermined end authoritatively prescribes one course of action in preference to another. In this sense the world offers itself to the agent as a boundless field of possibilities. The awareness of this freedom is tantamount to the discovery of all-engulfing Nought. The "abyss" of freedom is identical with the abyss of Nothingness. Standing with seeing eyes at the brink of this abyss means giddiness—a perverse emotional mixture of dread (a dread of Nothing) and longing. Becoming fully and anxiously aware of this desperate situation means to exist in the doubly sharpened sense of this word—not only to exist as men must exist but to exist with a full consciousness of man's terrible freedom. Existence is anguish (*Angst*). And stepping forth into a decision as we well must (for we are not free not to exercise our freedom) is an act of which no rational account can be given. All we can say of this experience in retrospect is either paradoxical or negative. Paradoxically we may describe choice as the liberation from the servitude of freedom. Or expressing it indirectly by showing what it is not, we may point out its being discontinuous with its own antecedents—a leap rather than a development, a breach rather than a continuation, a fall or a being lifted up rather than an advance.

There is still a third way of depicting the dénouement of the Existentialist "crisis of freedom." We may have recourse to God and believe that He intervenes through an act of grace, and in support of this interpretation, we may connect the idea of God's "total otherness" with the characteristic discontinuity of the Existentialist crisis. But in resorting to this interpretation, we overstep the limits of Existentialist thought. The breaking of the deadlock of absolute freedom, like every event discontinuous with its antecedents, escapes rational justification. At best it can be observed as a fact and hypothetically referred to an irrational power as its cause. Existential analysis by its very nature may become a preface to demonology, and accidentally only can it lead to Christian theology.

Wherever in modern thought we meet the configuration of the concepts just enumerated and briefly characterized —existence, absolute freedom, anxiety, and crisis—we identify the type of thinking before us as Existentialist. Barring superficial imitations, we may then assume that the spring of this thinking is found in an experience curiously on the verge between legitimate and universally accessible experience and pathological deviation—the Encounter with Nothingness.

"Existence precedes essence." So reads the simplest formula for Existentialism. This formula works only if the implied fusion of the three meanings of existence (the simple "being there," the human mode of being, the human mode of being combined with passionate self-consciousness) is accepted as an authentic notion. The contention of this philosophy is that the manifestation of freedom through which existence emerges—something out of nothing—is prior to essence, that is, to the determinations of both the status of the world and the nature of the human self. World and self (the region of essences) emerge only in consequence of the act of originating liberty (existence). If we call this act subjective and dub nihilistic any view that assigns centrality to the experience of Nothingness, we may assert: Existentialism is subjectivism in its passage through nihilism.

The components of Existentialism are before us. We now proceed to study it in action.

II

Nothingness Astir

THE FRENCH republic of letters, after being submerged for five years by war and occupation, gave a first sign of quickly recovered vitality by broadcasting the word Existentialism into a less resilient world. Reports on lectures given by Jean-Paul Sartre came across the ocean. We heard of police required to hold back the crowd surging into the lecture room, of the audience rising after the lecture like one man, determination in every heart. But what they were determined to do they did not know, for the lecturer had told them about their total freedom, and by offering advice as to a preferable course of action he would have encroached upon this freedom. Total freedom, he explained, was freedom to choose any course, and his sole counsel was: "Be your own counselor. Do what you please, but do it wholeheartedly."

With his novels Sartre conquered a reading audience and with his plays the stage, not only in Paris but also in London, New York, and Berlin. The work of other French writers pointed similar lessons and Existentialism became the watchword of a literary group. The name of Simone de Beauvoir was associated with that of Sartre, and Albert Camus seemed a more distant ally.

The observer may feel tempted to shrug off French Existentialism as just another short-lived literary fashion. In fact, Sartre's literary productions, though interesting and even brilliant, are anything but engaging. The air of decadence which pervades them and their preoccupation with diseased pleasures, lurid incidents, and promiscuous loves suggest cynicism rather than a constructive philosophy. They seem to reflect the misery only and not the grandeur of total freedom. But Sartre's achievements should not be measured by his imaginative writings. He offers his Existentialism as a system as austere and exacting in its conceptual architecture as the strictest traditionalist could wish. Especially his voluminous work on *Being and Nothingness* (*L'être et le néant*) shows no lack of either subtlety or rigor of thinking. It will be necessary to concede to this literary school a place in the development of contemporary philosophy.

The fact is that the Latin Quarter did not give birth to Existentialism. It was imported from Germany—a gift of the vanquished to the conqueror. The wave which lifted Sartre and his friends to notoriety had risen and thrown up an earlier crest in defeated Germany after the First World War. Karl Jaspers was its earliest spokesman. He was followed by Martin Heidegger, the most powerful mind in the movement. Sartre owes so much to this German precursor that his philosophy might be described as an ingenious and original adaptation and transformation of Heidegger's thought. But even during the twenty years' pause between the wars Existentialism was not confined to Germany. Miguel de Unamuno and Ortega y Gasset led a parallel movement in Spain, restoring the tragic significance of *Nada*, the Spanish idea of Nothingness as the vanity of even the greatest things, and in Italy Giovanni Gentile developed an activism which showed a considerable affinity to Existentialist thought. An Existentialist vanguard was active in France, publishing chiefly in the *Recherches Philosophiques*, an annual. And of the two important Russian exiles of the era, Nicolai Berdyaev and Leo Chestov, the former was akin to the Existentialists while the latter clearly belonged among their number.

In short, modern Existentialism was from its inception an affair of Western civilization rather than of any one particular nation. In the body of our ailing society, Existentialist language broke out like sore spots, indicating the centers of disturbance—pre-Nazi Germany, prerevolutionary Spain, France gathering strength after her débacle and threatened by a new one. England and America, less deeply shaken by the European upheaval, showed less responsiveness, and they still continue only mildly impressed. This observation casts no discredit on the philosophy in question, nor, of course, is it a recommendation. Disaster may teach wisdom, but it may also turn people's heads.

L'échappement à soi-même—the escape from oneself—is one of Sartre's favorite expressions. Existentialism itself is continually escaping from itself and wherever we meet it we find it in the process of becoming something else. There is no integral Existentialism, for obvious reasons. The thesis of total freedom excludes commitment to any particular cause while enjoining commitment to commitment, or the determination to be determined. Actually, however, it is not possible to engage in intelligent utterance without passing beyond that formal commitment and accepting the commitment to a material cause, a definable ideal. In order to speak, we must break the deadlock of the anguish of total freedom.

Accordingly, we find Heidegger embracing an eschatological neopaganism which he derives from Hölderlin's hymns. The commitment is here to "the gods of Being." Sartre avows faith in humanism. The commitment with him is to the universal idea of man—an idea difficult to maintain in the face of the Existentialist denial of a given "nature" or "essence" of man (Sartre, *L' existentialisme est un humanisme* [Paris, 1946], p. 70). But these are arbitrary choices. Once the Existentialist premises are conceded, it is just as easy to draw from them a variety of other conclusions—for example, the conclusions of racial nationalism or statism. But also communism (of the Sorel type) can be arrived at from the same point of departure. Nothingness, avid for a filling, is not fastidious. There is, however, one filling, one particular commitment which seems to be associated with Existentialism not only by arbitrary choice but by affinity. This is Christianity.

Wherever in this our "time of troubles" an Existentialist movement developed, it was paralleled by a Christian Existentialism. There was Gabriel Marcel in France, Theodor Haecker in Germany—both Catholics and thinkers of great depth and integrity. The impact on Protestantism was even greater. Karl Jaspers showed from the beginning strong Christian leanings and the Christian element in his thought has lately become more marked. But a much more important event in the recent history of Protestantism was the restoration of its theology under the influence of the Existentialist catalytic—the rise of a "theology of crisis" or "dialectical theology" led by Karl Barth and Emil Brunner. In its Protestant theological version, Existentialism has even secured a foothold in America, thanks to the work of Reinhold Niebuhr, who was influenced by Paul Tillich. Hardly less significant was the growth of a Jewish Existentialism represented chiefly by Franz Rosenzweig and Martin Buber.

The Existentialist idea of crisis bears a certain resemblance to the religious ideas of repentance, conversion, and spiritual rebirth. This apparently is the link between Existentialism and Christianity. We shall see whether this is a strong and durable link or an illusory one. But we should not even try to approach this question without remembering the initiator of Existentialist thought. Modern Existentialism, whether secular or religious, is a Kierkegaard renaissance.

Sören Kierkegaard died in 1855 in his native Copenhagen at the age of forty-two. His works, written in Danish, remained unknown outside his small country throughout the nineteenth century. The rediscovery began in the years preceding the disaster of 1914 with a translation into German. After World War I, Kierkegaard became a central figure in the contemporary scene and his presence gave rise to a new philosophy which he endowed with his own characteristic vocabulary. The Existentialist terms such as existence, crisis, dread, leap, total freedom, and the like are all of them borrowings from Kierkegaard.

Kierkegaard himself, however, did not consider his work a contribution to philosophy and, least of all, the foundation of a new school of thought. In writing on philosophical questions his chief aim was the denunciation of philosophy and philosophers, and this denunciation, it is true, required philosophical argument. His philosophical criticism (critical of all philosophy but especially of Hegel's) was subservient to a religious purpose. Kierke-

gaard desired to be a Christian and his Christian loyalty
gave meaning to his literary work—a work filled with the
passion of a great and tender soul. So the Christian mi-
nority alone among modern Existentialists is faithful to
Kierkegaard's intent, unless Kierkegaard misjudged himself. In fact, the complexity of his thought is such as to
cast doubt on his single-mindedness as a writer.

The Christian intent of Kierkegaard is clearly and
powerfully voiced in his religious addresses. With his
Works of Love, the *Discourses at the Communion on Fridays*,
and the address on *The Unchangeableness of God*, Kierkegaard belongs among the great Christian preachers. Certain oversharp accents and hyberbolisms of thought may
occasionally jar on the ear of a sensitive reader. He may,
for example, suspect some spiritual fastidiousness in
Kierkegaard's severing of charity or Christian love from
its moorings in natural love, which leads him to the
strange idea that deceased souls are the most appropriate
objects of purified love. But it would be unfair to dwell on
the minor disturbances of balance in the otherwise rich
and powerful whole of Kierkegaard's religious thought.

However, it was not the Christian theology of the discourses that awoke to life in the Existentialist movement.
Aside from expressing his faith directly in the traditional
language of devotion, Kierkegaard chose to further his
cause by an indirect expression. The writings following
this indirect method were published under quaint pseudo-
nyms. There was, of course, never any doubt as to their
authorship. But by failing to sign them with his real name,
Kierkegaard served notice to his readers that the point
of view adopted in them was not his own point of view
but that he merely experimented with it.

The pseudonymous books do not express faith. In them

a number of fictitious and rather vaguely imagined characters speak from the standpoint of unbelief, varying,
however, in proximity to faith. The views expressed range
from desperate agnosticism and diabolical sensualism (all
the more diabolical for its lack of animal spirits, its de-
liberate coldness) to an attitude which is almost and yet
not entirely faith. The tenets of faith are accepted, but
tentatively only, in an experimenting spirit, as something
that might be so but might conceivably also be otherwise.
They reflect possibilities. The shadow of Nothingness is
upon them.

The experimenting mind suffers a painful suspense. It
is caught in indecision, it has no real foothold, it cannot
stay where it is. Nor can it move on to a new position, for
the only two ways out of its predicament are barred. One
way out would consist in surrendering faith altogether and
deafen the voice of conscience (that is, the desire for a
foothold, a leverage to unhinge the world) with the loud
pleasures of the world. But the voice, with still insistence,
makes itself audible through the clamor of affairs and the
numbness of surfeited senses. The "aesthetic life" is no
possible solution. Nor does the other way out seem viable.
Our reason, far from leading us along an ascending road
to God, shows us only the absurdity of the affirmations of
faith. So we are lost and undone, equally unable to believe
and not to believe. Only a miracle can save us. Then the
unhappy experimenter, with the astringent voice of despair, dares God (in case He should exist) to perform the
miracle and to ravish him to His breast by the gift of faith.
Faith is to be achieved "by virtue of the absurd." The
encounter with Nothingness is to shock the soul into the
presence of God. But, of course, this effect must not be
counted upon. It is a mere possibility.

In the mind of their author, also the imaginative-analytic writings with their experimenting approach serve the religious purpose. They too are a preparation for the Gospel (*praeparatio evangelica*), but of a novel kind. By their indirectness they are designed to spare the freedom of the reader. Their author does not claim for himself any religious authority, and they do not burst into the adytum of the soul with blunt assertions. They do not say: "This is so! Believe that!" Instead they involve the reader's mind in an experimenting search and help him establish that terrible and yet, as Kierkegaard believes, salutary, balance between two apparent impossibilities—the impossibility of unbelief and the impossibility of faith. "My whole life is an epigram calculated to make people aware," Kierkegaard notes in the *Journals* (1848). And he compares his method with the Socratic midwifery which, instead of engendering thought, helps others in the delivery of intellectual offspring.

We may wonder, however, whether the subtle justification of the indirect method tells the whole story. The very nature of faith militates against its use. Where there is faith, it will make itself heard in no uncertain language. The inner compulsion to bear witness will override all scruples regarding the speaker's authority. Religious truth is that light which will not be put under a bushel. So in St. Paul's First Epistle to the Corinthians, the praise of love is followed immediately by the injunction to speak out clearly: "For if the trumpet give an uncertain sound, who shall prepare himself for the battle?" (II Cor. 14:8). Kierkegaard himself, in the *Works of Love*, shows great eagerness "to make love secure." Love, eternally confirmed by God as a duty, he writes there, drives out all anguish and it even becomes purged of the longing for tests and trials, so sure is it of itself. Yet throughout the pseudonymous writings love is on trial: the story of Abraham's sacrifice is given a key position. And all this pitiless testing of love is permeated by anguish. Love seems not secure and despair lurks behind it.

So the concern for the freedom of others, however real for Kierkegaard, is a legitimate but not a sufficient explanation of his indirect method of apologetics. The fact is that the writer with one part of his being actually lives on the level of uncertainty or merely hypothetical faith. Those shadowy characters of his are impersonations of his own self, repudiated by the real Kierkegaard yet not entirely disavowed: they are granted expression. He conforms to his own definition of a poet as "an unhappy being whose heart is torn by secret sufferings, but whose lips are so strangely formed that when the sighs and the cries escape them, they sound like beautiful music" (*Either/Or*, I, 15). That secret suffering (not kept very secret in this case) which moves the poet Kierkegaard to utterance is the wound suffered in the encounter with Nothingness. Kierkegaard has many names both for this experience and the spiritual disease induced by it. It is best described as irony—the attitude of one who can play with everything because he is committed to nothing. It is negative freedom. Everything the ironical man touches is overspread with the eerie aspect of mere possibility and thereby ceases to be nourishing spiritual food. In his magisterial dissertation Kierkegaard portrays allegedly Socrates but actually his own person as the demon of irony surrounding himself with the desert of Nothingness.

Aside from being a poet, Kierkegaard is a philosophical

analyst. The confrontation with Nothingness becomes for him a dialectical problem. His problem—by its nature an insoluble one—is: How can the void of Nothingness be filled? How can something come of nothing? How can total freedom, conversant as it is with possibilities only, become total commitment under a constraining reality? As a young man, living under the spell of irony, Kierkegaard notes in the confession of Gilleleie (*Journals*, 1 August 1835), "true knowledge must begin with un-knowing, in the same way in which God created the world out of nothing." Analogy, the chief constructive principle of Christian theology, is here disastrously misapplied. Man, differing therein from God, must begin with Being that circumscribes him, or else, by attributing to himself God's freedom, he bids fair to play the role of the miserable godling, the frustrated Titan, Prometheus, at odds not with the tyrannical Zeus but with God Father Almighty.

There is in the pseudonymous works a surplus which the subtlest strategy of soul-winning is unable to justify. In these dialectical-poetical outpourings, we find Kierkegaard locked in combat with the unsubdued demons in his own breast. The battle seems inconclusive and neither victory nor defeat is in sight. Because of the inconclusiveness of the Kierkegaardian dialectic, the relationship between the religious addresses and the dialectical writings is an ambiguous one. Instead of reinforcing each other, they are weakened by their dubious parallelism. The addresses, considered in the light of the pseudonymous works, may appear as a brilliant rhetorical display of an experimentally adopted faith. While this one-sided view is grossly unfair to Kierkegaard, the alternative, though less offensive, is equally unsatisfactory. Looked at from the point of view of the addresses, that is, from

the point of view of unquestioning faith, it is impossible
to justify the poetical-dialectical exercises with their
suspense of faith as a subtle form of evangelization. They
must rather appear as an audacious play with the temptation of despair which may prompt some to take heed
while corrupting others.

Perhaps we are overstating the contradiction in Kierkegaard's thought, but be that as it may, what has hap-
pened to his work in our own time must surely give pause
to his Christian admirers. Existentialism is largely a
resurrection of the dialectician Kierkegaard. In the modern replica of his work, his doubts seem greater than his
faith. Sartre is like one of the fictitious characters of the
pseudonymous books come to life. Man as reasoner is to
imitate God in beginning with Nothing, so reads Kierkegaard's suggestion. Taken up and recast by Sartre, it
becomes a manifesto of integral atheism. The liberals,
Sartre charges, abolished God but inconsistently retained
divine laws. We must think atheism through and conceive of man as having the power to make something out
of nothing, to confer meaning upon meaningless life and
to invent values. But where is the seriousness of values
if we have to invent them? "To this I reply," Sartre
writes, "that I am very sorry that such is the case. But
since I have discarded God the Father, someone is needed
to invent values" (*L'existentialisme, etc.*, p. 89). Kierkegaard's experimentation is resumed, and of his two apparent impossibilities—the impossibility of unbelief and
the impossibility of faith—the former is found less impossible.

We are oversimplifying the picture if we think of Existentialism as a drama in two acts. First Kierkegaard,
and then after a lengthy pause the resuscitation of Kierke-

gaard. Kierkegaard, though long overlooked by Europe,
was yet a son of the Western world and his work was its
seasonal fruit. The encounter with Nothingness was expressed by him with the unmatched intellectual radical-
ism and precision of the dialectician who had gone
through Hegel's school. But the experience as such, far
from being unique with him, was symptomatic of the
romantic malady as it afflicted the second generation.
Kierkegaard was a kinsman of E. T. A. Hoffmann, Schopenhauer, Heine, Keats, Musset, and above all of Leopardi.

The despair over an unresponsive and meaningless
world, the turning away from it towards a dreamland
which is only a painted veil covering Primal Negation,
death longed for with voluptuousness, a beauty whose
sight sears the eye, a truth that withers the heart, a love
which destroys the beloved one, a greatness of soul which
is paralyzed by languor and disfigured by the blemish
of a guilt past repentance and redemption—all these
somber inventions of contemporary imagination haunt
Kierkegaard's anonymous writings. In mythological or
historical garb, impersonating Nero, Don Juan, Faust,
mermen and necromancers, suicides and maniacs, the
spirits of this romantic nether world suffer the curse of
their futile existence, holding tryst in sickly moonlight,
under the flickering lamps of a stale banquet or in the
deceptive dawn of the small hours, shunning broad
daylight.

In the eyes of the poet who invoked this phantasma-
goria, nothing is more shocking to reason, more incredible
than the Incarnation. In fact, this Christian mystery has
become altogether unapproachable. For the problem is now
not how to make room in nature for supernature but how
to dislodge the demons claiming the world for themselves.

With the majority of his contemporaries Kierkegaard drew upon the romantic experience, and he shared the fate of the problematic personality typical of his century. Their peculiar fight was "the battle of demons." The intellectual disorder which generally attends moral struggle—the struggle of all times—deepened so that not only the outcome but the meaning of the struggle grew doubtful. The good suffered a sea-change and took on the aspect of evil; evil appeared intellectually more attractive than good; truth ceased to be an ally of virtue, and the belief in God and a rationally ordered world offered itself as a temptation, a cowardly refuge into comfortable illusion. The minds were touched by the charm of the weird sister: "Fair is foul, and foul is fair." Courage demanded rebellion. When Nietzsche, the problematic man *par excellence*, proclaimed that God was dead, he intended a deed of utmost bravery. Man dared to live as one having no hope, and without God in the world—to assert himself in the face of Nothingness. This seemed heroism, and Karl Jaspers recognized in Nietzsche the cofounder of Existentialism.

The "battle of the demons" raged with greatest fury in the minds of Russian intellectuals. Unrestrained by the Christian-Humanist tradition of the West and intoxicated by their newly acquired intellectual freedom, they seized upon Hegelian dialectic as a method by which to think out extreme possibilities. Negation, the dynamic element in Hegel's system, was given unlimited range. The theoretical negation included practical negation. Under the Russian Caesaropapism (the union of secular and ecclesiastical power in an absolute monarch) the thinking, that is, free, personality became inevitably an enemy of the existing order, just as in the preceding century the religious personalities had been driven into a hermitage. Intellectual life resembled a sweet, strong potion dangerous to both body and soul. To be an intellectual was tantamount to being a nihilist, though the nihilist, in frequent cases, turned a Christian convert. Bakunin thought and lived the idea of creative destruction as the manifestation of man's divine freedom. Bjelinski, champion of Russian liberalism, said: "The negation is my goddess." Dostoyevsky's novels, finally, swarm with incarnations of nihilism. We remember Ivan in the *Brothers Karamazov* with his nihilist profession of faith: "God does not exist. Hence everything is allowed;" or Kirillov, in *The Possessed*, who tries to achieve the deification of man by suicide as a supreme assertion of freedom; or the hero of the same novel, Stavrogin: if a man gifted with the vision of a Byron or Lermontov tried to rewrite Kierkegaard's portrait of Nero, combining it with that of Don Juan, he might arrive at Dostoyevsky's Stavrogin.

There are some Teutonic elements in the work of Sartre, leader of French Existentialism. But there is even more in it that seems Russian. The situation in which Sartre conceived his philosophy paralleled the prerevolutionary Russian situation. The foreign tyranny of Nazi occupation had forced the mind into the role of the resister. To think meant to deny the existing order. Accordingly, the poetical symbols in Sartre's writings tend to identify free action with destruction, as for example, with matricide in *The Flies*. *Néantisation* (Heidegger's *Nichtung*), "nihilation," is, according to Sartre's analysis, the characteristic achievement of that nothingness (*néant*) which is man. Nihilation, he holds, is at the basis of his experiencing the world and himself. In his construction of houses and cities, destruction, the aim of war, is already latent.

Modern Existentialism is the quintessence of the nihilistic poison exuded by the ailing mind of Europe. Every medicine is a poison. "Swallow this finest poison, and you will get well," is the Existentialist's counsel.

III

Estrangement

LOOKED AT FROM this side of the Atlantic, Existentialism appears a bewildering phenomenon. Metaphysical systems, especially of the idealistic German type, are generally eyed with suspicion. Their offense consists in propounding high-sounding and vast ideas which impress the level-headed and practically minded man as unscientific. Existentialism too has this soaring quality together with a lack of appreciation of science and progress. But, in addition, it succeeds in paradoxically combining the familiar defect with one diametrically opposed to it—the scandalous repudiation of ideas which every sane person is expected to hold. It offends healthy skepticism by metaphysical impetus while at the same time disturbing naive faith by fierce negations. Its paradoxical name, "theology without God," sums up well its twofold offensiveness. For people are inclined to believe in God but seldom go so far as to tolerate theology.

People feel bewildered by Existentialism because they are fortunate or inexperienced enough not to have encountered Nothingness. They are especially unacquainted with the experience of estrangement which means the encounter with the Nothingness of the world. To be

estranged is tantamount to living in a world without signs
—an alarming experience similar to that of a person
transported to a strange place with no visible markings
or legible road signs. Actually a world without signs is
something less than a world—a mere congeries of obtrusive
existents. So the experience in question may also be described as the obliteration of world in the sense of a
meaningful and familiar totality.

It is unwise to dismiss the experience of estrangement
as morbid or decadent. The question of man's relationship
to the world is posed to everyone at every time. Every
living man has his answer to this question though he may
not be able to formulate it. His life is the answer. It makes
a fundamental difference to our mode of life whether we
look upon the world as something like a home, a station
on the way home, a testing ground, an arsenal of potential
tools, a quarry supplying material to the human workman,
a foreign country, an enemy camp, or a prison. All these
possibilities have been tried out at one time or another in
practice as well as in theory. The failure to make the
question articulate may tempt us into accepting two contradictory answers without noticing their disparity. We
may, for example, think "with the top of our minds" of
the world as something like a comfortable and nearly
homelike quarry, while deeper down there sits the fear
that the metaphor of the enemy camp might be more
fitting. The suspicion lurks at the bottom of the tech-
nologist's mind that this quarry world of ours, this successfully manipulated material, has a nasty way of hitting
back at Prometheus—at man the artificer.

It is better to have one philosophy though it be a faulty
one, than several philosophies incompatible with each
other. The champions of estrangement deserve our grati-

tude for forcing us to face the problem and make up our minds. Existentialism is an antidote against smug confusion. Its exponents, however, recommend it as a regular fare, and this a different matter.

In a book which once served as a primer to Western man in the infancy of his civilization and which is now recovering its relevance, because once more philosophers have a fair chance to be thrown in prison—in Boethius' *Consolation of Philosophy*—a prisoner is given comfort by Dame Philosophy. The prisoner's mind is disturbed by a tragic cleavage which, it seems to him, separates man from nature. Nature imperturbably revolves in her grooves. Why, then, is human life allowed to get out of joint? This is a question suggested by estrangement. Dame Philosophy counters with her great alternative: "Do you think that the world is driven by wild and fortuitous happenings, or do you believe there is in it some rule of reason" (I prose 6, 4–6)? Are there "signs" for our orientation which make a world out of this huge welter of events? The question in Boethius is supposed to admit of one reply only. The prisoner is not expected to carry impious despair to the point of absurdity. Surely he must agree that there are traces of "some rule of reason." His is but a light case of estrangement and it is easily cured.

Philosophy as the Greeks conceived it is one single effort of the human mind to interpret the system of signs and so to relate man to the world as a comprehensive order within which a place is assigned to him. Man may either fill that place properly or he may miss it. Because of the terrible risk of error and failure, it is of the utmost importance to read the signs correctly. Safe lights must be distinguished from will-o'-the-wisps. Otherwise we may fall into disastrous errors, maintaining, for example, that might makes right because in animal life the stronger rules by tooth and claw. The ancient masterpiece of the art of reading the signs is Plato's *Timaeus*. In this philosophical prose poem the world appears as a marvelous device of Reason for our instruction. Through observing the unperturbed and perfect motions of the heavens, we learn how to establish order in the disturbed and erring movements of our own mind. This Hellenic cosmos can be reinterpreted as God's creation. The Christian thinkers who effect this translation base themselves on a word of St. Paul. Pointing out that the language of signs is legible to everyone, gentile and Jew alike, the apostle affirms that "the invisible things of God" (His divinity which sets the distinction between right and wrong) are yet visible to the mind "through the things created" (Rom. 1:20). The signs, theologically speaking, are the vestiges of God in the created world.

One may be more or less sanguine in the appraisal of available signs. The dissenters from the *philosophia perennis* (the Platonic-Aristotelian and Christian tradition) do not carry their protest to the point of denying signs altogether. They merely suggest an alternative and less ambitious reading. For Lucretius Carus, for example, the enthusiastic expositor of Epicurus' teachings, the unbiased study of nature results in a moral lesson. Every living being, the lesson reads, is fated to die. Hence we should learn from nature to accept mortality, that is, our own imminent extinction. The void which is mixed into all things as their past nonexistence and their future nonexistence should be acquiesced in. Compared with the Platonic-Christian idea of a purposeful universe, the scope of Nothingness is allowed to expand. But it is still contained by scientific insight into the nature of things.

Much the same is true of contemporary naturalism, the philosophy dominant especially in America. Its opposition to metaphysical or supernatural thought is that of a competitor in the interpretation of signs. Evolution, the key feature of reality according to the naturalist view, is regarded as a pointer. Through it nature supposedly shows us in which direction we ought to move and, by nature's decree, shall move. The sign in this case is a particularly unsatisfactory one, because only in a circuitous way does it apply to the individual and his problems. Yet thanks to its temporary conformity with a technological and political development, this naturalistic sign-reading can enlist popular devotion. Still in our own time, after two destructive world wars, it furnishes the hardly shaken foundation of faith in progress. Faulty sign-reading has here hit upon an element of truth which the critics of faith in progress are in danger of overlooking. The idea of progress follows not from an evolutionary trend in the nature of things (to believe that is to indulge in bad metaphysics), but it flows from the responsibility devolving upon man with his narrowly restricted but infinitely important role as the maker of his world of tools and social institutions.

In any case, men everywhere and at all times, though with varying success and a vision more or less clouded by their self-assertiveness and little-mindedness, recognize signs which confer upon the vast multitude of experienced facts the character of a world. This consent of the nations is challenged by Existentialism, a philosophy that denies signs altogether and conceives of man's status amidst reality as that of a total stranger. It holds that, considered in themselves, the things around us are meaningless; that they have no message for us; that knowledge does not

lead to wisdom. Ancient skepticism pales in comparison
with so drastic a negation. Measured by it, the freethinkers
of the eighteenth century appear naive believers and our
Pragmatists, Positivists, and Naturalists stand revealed as
stodgy conservatives in matters of creed.

It was Kant who paved the way to the Primal Negation.
The intent of his philosophy was construction, or rather
reconstruction. The effective reading of signs was to be
restored in the face of skepticism and materialism which
claimed to offer the adequate philosophical interpretation
of Newtonian physics, so destroying in the name of science
the means for moral orientation. Kant tried to show that
science does not actually oust man from an understandable
world, and he redefined his place in it. However, he
achieved his purpose at an enormous sacrifice by confin-
ing man's knowledge to the phenomenal world. In order
to make room for faith, he debarred reason as a human
faculty from grasping the "thing in itself." He divorced
knowledge from reality. So great was the impact of his
verdict of separation upon the minds of his readers (and
soon the educated all over the Western world were his
readers), that Hegel, in a countermove, conceived the
work of knowledge as an act of reconciliation. This term
as Hegel used it was fraught with religious meaning. It
signified the marriage of spirit and matter, the latter
shedding its brute factuality and revealing itself as a
materialization of spirit. It also suggested the absorption
of the distraught and rebellious mind into the peace of
God. Hegel's Dionysian logic of reconciliation claimed to
vibrate in the rhythm of the divine life manifest in the
world, and to give effect, in the sphere of thought, to the
mystery of Incarnation.

Against this stupendous claim Kierkegaard lodges

his protest—the protest of the unreconciled individual. "Knowledge of reality is not reconciliation to reality, and speculation is not salvation"—this was the Kierkegaardian countermove, or rather counterblast, to Hegel's anti-Kantian countermove. From the dizzy height of speculative ecstasy the mind plunged into the depth of utter forlornness. Kierkegaard's experience of estrangement resembled an awakening from the Hegelian dream (not the reality) of the mystic union of the soul with the World Spirit—from a vision for which the fundamental difference between Creation and Incarnation was lost in the hybrid idea of a dialectic-cosmic theophany. After this rapture, contact with reality meant mortification. The experience of estrangement articulated itself against the background of a fading pantheistic trance.

Kierkegaard's *Journals* show several entries under the same date, May 12, 1839. In the first, Incarnation and Creation are seen as corresponding events, the former being in the world of spirit what the latter is in the physical world. From these premises a daring conclusion is drawn regarding the Holy Spirit as the food of the Spiritual World. A cataclysm seems to have occurred between this entry and the following one which reads: "The whole reality terrifies me, from the smallest fly to the mysteries of Incarnation. Everything in it is inexplicable to me, most of all my own self. The whole reality is pestiferous to me, most of all my own self. Great is my sorrow, unlimited. . . ." Then, in *Repetition* (1843) we find the classic expression of estrangement:

One sticks one's finger into the soil to tell by the smell in what land one is: I stick my finger into existence—it smells of nothing. Where am I? Who am I?

How came I here? What is this thing called the world? What does this word mean? Who is it that has lured me into the thing, and now leaves me there? . . . How did I come into the world? Why was I not consulted, why not made acquainted with its manners and customs but was thrust into the ranks as though I had been bought of a kidnapper, a dealer in souls? How did I obtain an interest in this big enterprise they call reality? Why should I have an interest in it? Is it not a voluntary concern? And if I am compelled to take part in it, where is the director? . . . Whither shall I turn with my complaint? Existence is surely a debate— may I beg that my view be taken into consideration? If one is to take the world as it is, would it not be better never to learn what it is? (Pp. 114 ff. This and the other quotations from Kierkegaard are used by permission of the Princeton University Press and the American-Scandinavian Foundation.)

With the air which we inhale through our nostrils we become most intimately, in a physical and more than physical sense, part of the surrounding world. This intimacy is destroyed in an estranged world—it smells of nothing. Nothingness cannot be affirmed—it cannot be said to be; therefore the array of unanswered questions. There are no signs. Especially there is absence of that sign which furnishes the clue to all other signs. This master sign is "the Good," the end or purpose for the sake of which things exist and which must include man's good or purpose, the answer to his existential interrogative "Why?" When Descartes tries out idealism in considering reality as a compound of ideas in the mind, he experiments with the hypothesis of a malignant and all-powerful demon who might have put these ideas into our minds although they corresponded to no reality. When Kierkegaard, going far beyond the idealistic doubt, envisages an estranged world, the nightmare of the omnipotent demon presents itself again. But meanwhile, the malevolence of the demon has deepened into satanic wickedness. He does not only withhold reality (we might come to terms with an orderly illusion) but defrauds us of its purpose and thus condemns us to misery. Continuing that jesting and yet serious quest of the "director," Kierkegaard writes: "What is a deceiver? Does not Cicero say that a deceiver can be found out by asking the question *cui bono?*—for whose good?" The "director" of the great enterprise is under suspicion of being a fraud.

Contemporary Existentialist literature is haunted by the vision of an estranged world. K., the hero in Franz Kafka's *The Castle*, is a stranger in the snowbound village (the world) which lies in mysterious subjection to the unapproachable lord of the castle. Albert Camus, in *The Stranger*, shows the passage of an individual through crime and punishment which do not touch him, as though he were a shadow flitting across the indifferent earth. For the chief character in Sartre's *La Nausée*, things take on an aspect of obscene violence: they are there, shamelessly exhibited, reveling in existence, pullulating, and, as it were, glorying in the senselessness of their factuality. As dread reveals the estrangement of the world, so nausea is symptomatic of the estrangement of the human body: his own hands resting on the table before him seem to the patient like two crouching, mysteriously tentacled animals. The Orestes of the same writer, in *The Flies*, suffers from a similar plight: he is an exile even in his native Argos, and always has been one, even in his boyhood. In W. H. Auden's "Christmas Oratorio," estrangement is symbolized by the winter night with "darkness and snow" descending "upon all personality," and finally, in T. S. Eliot, we have the cruelly striking imagery of the "waste land," "the place of disaffection." But the credit for giving the idea of estrangement a rigorous philosophical expression goes to Martin Heidegger.

In Heidegger's *Sein und Zeit*, the fragmentary main work of modern Existentialist philosophy, man is depicted as "thrown into the world," which vaguely recalls a delinquent thrown into prison. And in fact he appears guilty, in a sense which empties this term of its moral significance. Man's guilt does not consist in the infraction of a law, nor must the term be understood in a moral sense. It rather denotes man's status, his "ek-sistence" as a "being outside himself" with that which he is not—with the world. In self-alienation man surrenders himself unto a world which in turn is alien to him. Homelessness, according to Heidegger, is not the exceptional condition of one who has been deprived of his country and his relatives. It rather describes the fundamental aspect of the world which persists, though it can be overlaid for the individual by a veneer of familiarity. But privation logically precedes affirmation and man's being-at-home must be interpreted as a modification of his original forlornness, and this order is irreversible. The assertion of the "unhomelikeness" of the world is even stronger than the English rendition can suggest, because the German word (*Unheimlichkeit*) carries the notion of the uncanny, gruesome, and insidiously mysterious.

Heidegger's world closes round man like a prison, and yet it is a self-imprisonment which he suffers. The foreignness of the world is man's alienation from himself—an alienation which is not his accidental defect but the fundamental defectiveness of his nature. Man projects his own temporality (he is essentially time) onto the screen of Nothingness. Thanks to this flight and defection from himself, he has world. And this world of his interposes itself between his ego and Nothingness. To it he may cling as to his shelter and arsenal of tools and call it home in the cowardly refusal to recognize its transparency towards Nought. The illusion of a homelike world is the anguished flight of the mind from that encounter with Nothingness towards which it moves as its own ineluctable end. This end is death. Deliverance from illusion is to be achieved by the man who, opening himself to anguish, resolutely faces Nothingness in anticipation of his own extinction. Heidegger's astonishing book, of which these remarks give only a coarsened and approximate idea, is truly the philosophical monument of the breathing space between two of the greatest slaughters of all history. It is perfumed with the exhalations of death. Like the uniform of the black guard, it is marked all over with the mortuary emblem of skull and bones. How, in fact, can foreignness be brought home to the living more forcefully than by intimacy with death?

The city of Argos, in Sartre's *The Flies*, is a place where the dead are more alive than the living. Its usurper king, Aegisthus, expresses the experience of estrangement thus: "It is neither sad nor gay, the desert, the innumerable nothingness of sand under the luminous nothingness of the sky: it is sinister. Oh, I would give my kingdom for being able to shed one tear" (II, 4).

Plato, expressing a conviction deeply rooted in the minds of his fellow Greeks, called the cosmos an ever liv-

ing animal and a visible god. When in the decline of
Hellenic civilization belief in the cosmos was shaken, the
Gnostic religion, penetrating from Mesopotamia and Syria
into the eastern marches of the Mediterranean world,
attempted a radical transvaluation of values, and it was
particularly successful where it posed as the Christian
heresy called Manichaeanism. In the anguished vision of
Gnostic mythology, the divinely ordered universe was
transformed into a dungeon. The Father of Light was
acquitted of the responsibility for creating it and the role
of the demiurge was allotted to an evil demon. The stars
in their orbits no longer proclaimed the rational wonders
of a celestial mathematics, but their malignant light
traced the weary round of the demonic prison guards
holding watch on the ramparts of the world. Meanwhile,
deep down in the pit, in the solitary confinement of its
prison cell, the spirit of man languished, oppressed by the
darkness of the senses and lashed by the lusts of the flesh.

The fading from man's mind of the idea of creation in
the modern era is a less dramatic event than the parallel
development in antiquity, and no equally drastic reversal
has been attempted. Yet there is in the Heideggerian
conception of the world an unmistakable reflection of the
demoniacal universe of the Gnostics. Even some of the
terms used by Heidegger sound as though they were
quoted from Gnostic documents, especially the idea of
man's being "thrown" into the world and the idea of
a "call" reaching him in his place of banishment. However, while Gnosticism promises to its followers liberation
through the Paraclete, who, coming from outside, will
victoriously break through the multiplied fortifications of
the universe and find and unchain the soul, the modern
teacher of estrangement knows no outside except Nothing-

ness and no deliverance except through annihilation. The Gnostics, drunken though they were with the riotous and sordid fancywork of their demonic cosmology, yet told their believers: we bid you hope. The contemporary Existentialist bids us to live without hope, but in freedom, a stranger to the world, but voluntarily so.

Men understand each other through a world common to all, or at least, common to all members of the community within which mutual understanding takes place. Minds meet only when a meeting place is provided by objects on which views can be exchanged. An estranged world, that is, one which is mute to the question Why?, destroys communion and condemns the individual to solitude. He may conceal his isolation with voluble speech and effusive companionableness. For, of course, there will be things enough left to talk about: things to be enjoyed, used, or made together. There will be a sphere of public interest and public discourse. But this communication will not develop into communion, nor the sharing of purposes into an accord of lives. For under the dispensation of estrangement, the supreme end, indicated by the master sign of the good, is missing. Gone is the co-ordinating principle that fits together things into a world and co-operative efforts into a fellowship of hearts. That which really matters remains ineffable. Therefore, any verbal expression of estrangement is ultimately defeated by that which it tries to express. Expression means sharing with others. But it is just as impossible to express estrangement with a view to sharing it as it is impossible to express, say, drowsiness with vivacity. Only indirectly, with reference to what it is not, can estrangement be enunciated.

Estrangement involves loneliness. It holds the individual in solitary confinement within the impervious walls of his individuality. Kierkegaard has an untranslatable term for this condition, rendered in the Princeton translation with "reservedness" but literally meaning "being locked up within oneself." To this inwardness of despair communication presents itself as an impossible achievement caught up as it is in this dilemma: Suppose we confine understanding to objects unrelated to an ultimate meaning or purpose. We then may achieve agreement as to how, for instance, a war should be fought, while we suspend judgment as to whether it is good to fight a war or this war now. This type of understanding, while presenting no insuperable difficulties, fails to break down the walls of solitude. Suppose, then, we include in our expression of thought the reference to an ultimate meaning or purpose. This inclusion may enable us to affirm that it is good to fight this war because it serves the defense of a possession more valuable than life. But by hypothesis (for we presuppose estrangement with no sign fixing the nature of the good) this meaning or purpose is arbitrarily chosen. Hence, expressing it and bringing it to bear on an interpretation of facts for the benefit of others is no true communication either. Communication requires reciprocity. Instead, utterance becomes that encroachment upon the freedom of one's fellow man which we call propaganda or indoctrination. The currency obtained in our time by these two odious words is a danger signal indicating the breakdown of communication. Estrangement involves a disintegration of society. Not the hermit in the African desert is the symbol of solitude in an estranged world but:

The desert is squeezed in the tube-train next to you,
The desert is in the heart of your brother.
                                        —T. S. Eliot, "The Rock"

The social nature of estrangement is Karl Marx's discovery. As a political writer and economist, he directed
his criticism against capitalist society and its fundamental
institution, private property. But for Marx, the philosopher, who speaks to us chiefly in his earlier writings,
capitalism is merely one aspect, though a very important
one, of a wider phenomenon: it expresses man's estrangement from his world.

Kierkegaard, we remember, discovered the meaninglessness of the world through a fall from the height of
Hegel's philosophy of reconciliation with the world. Similarly Marx discovered estrangement against the foil of
society as man's true homestead. Society, for him, is the
essential unity of man and nature. Society produces the
true man. But man must work in order to live, wresting
a livelihood from an as yet unreconciled nature. In working and making things, he externalizes himself. What
exists first as thought and plan in his mind, a part of
himself, becomes an object outside himself. So work is self-
estrangement: the thing becomes the maker's. As though
it were a bit of his self, he claims it as his own, to the
exclusion of claims which might be made upon it by his
fellows. But thereby he, the maker, comes under the sway
of the thing made. As a manifestation of the cleavage in
his mind, private property arises, and the individual falls
away from society. The process of estrangement begins.
Capitalism is the consummation of this process: the perfection of private property and total estrangement. Everything now has a price, nothing a value. The victim of
estrangement is the proletarian, man in the role of a
commodity. His life is a "filled nothing" which at any
moment threatens to fall into the "total nothingness" of
annihilation (*Nationalökonomie und Philosophie* [Kröners

Taschenausgabe], 1,362 ff.). But the curse of estrangement afflicts all members of society, even those who find
it enjoyable. It estranges man from man, and man from
his world. Instead of his physical and spiritual senses, he
has one sense only which holds the others in subjection:
the sense of having, which is the estrangement of all
senses and the reduction of man to a status of absolute
poverty (1,300).

A man working on an assembly line, making he knows
not what for he knows not whom, nor caring in the least,
next to his elbow a fellow worker whom he does not know
(tomorrow it will be someone else), earning just enough
to enable him to rise in the morning to return to his
place on the assembly line, enough also to make him
shoulder, hour by hour, all the empty time that is still
ahead of him, and to throw away as much of this burden
as he can upon unenjoyable pleasures, his cheap narcotics
—such is Marx's symbol of estrangement. This is the
unadorned void. The gilt void meanwhile haunts the
luxurious office, the suburban mansion, the opera house
where a singer sells his voice at so high a price that he
can afford to forget about that which is priceless in music.

Marx, however, was very far from teaching Existentialism. For him estrangement was not the status of man's
natural existence but merely a phase, though a necessary
one, of man's historical life. According to him, the path
of mankind inevitably leads through this void in order
then to rise, through the revolutionary crisis, to "perfect
Humanism," the first authentic incarnation of humanity
in communist society. It is well known to what extent
Marx succeeded in imparting his hope to the members
of the society which he criticized. It is less well known to
what extent his diagnosis of man's status was accepted by

those who rejected his hope and repudiated his plan of action. The encounter with Nothingness, for Marx a socio-political crisis, the birth pangs of a new man in a new society, becomes for his bourgeois disciples the fate of man as such, with some even a triumphant achievement, the consummation of his freedom. So for Sartre, *Il n'y a pas de signes dans le monde*—"there are no signs in the world," he affirms. And he concludes: therefore man is free (*L'existentialisme, etc.*, p. 47).

The counterpart in Heidegger to Marx's social idea of estrangement is the world as the superficial prattle and anonymous publicity reflect it—the world defined by that which "one" (*man*) thinks, judges, feels, opines. Even more revealing is a comparison of Marx's concept of "having" with that developed by Sartre. The emphasis in Sartre, rather than on externalization and estrangement, is on appropriation and assimilation to the self. Reading Marx backward, Sartre translates "I become my property" into "my property becomes (part of) myself." But the self is a void amidst the density of Being—the "hole" of Nothingness. Hence, "destruction realizes—more subtly perhaps than creation—the nature of appropriation, for the object is no longer there to show its impenetrability" (*L'être et le néant*, p. 683). The flames consuming the farm that I have set afire fuse that farm most intimately with myself. Generally speaking, the consumer is the owner in his most revealing role. And since desire, in the last analysis, desires nothing less than the whole world, an insignificant enjoyment such as the consuming of tobacco may take on a frightful symbolic significance. "Through the tobacco which I smoked it was the world that burned, that allowed itself to be smoked, that resolved itself into vapor to revert

into me" (*ibid.*, p. 687). The placid pipe is lighted by
M. Sartre with apocalyptic flames.

A system of signs, conceived as a structural feature
of reality, constitutes order. An habitable and homelike
world (even though the home be only a temporary one)
must first of all be an orderly world. Through the intellect
this order is discovered; through the will it is appropriated
and conferred upon action. Throughout millenniums of the
history of mankind, thinkers and saints did not waver in
awarding to order a divine rank. They regarded it not
as a contrast to freedom but rather as its indispensable
condition. Even the creative passion of love must submit
to order, the Franciscan poet taught. Echoing the Song
of Songs (II,4), as many Christian writers did before
him, he wrote:

> Set Love in order, thou that lovest Me.
> Never was virtue out of order found;
> And though I fill thy heart desirously,
> By thine own virtue I must keep My ground:
> When to My love thou dost bring charity,
> Even she must come with order girt and gown'd.
> Look how the trees are bound
> To order, bearing fruit;
> And by one thing compute,
> In all things earthly, order's grace or gain.
> —*Amor de caritade*, trans. by D. G. Rossetti

The praise of order is countered in Sartre with hatred
of order. Jupiter, in *The Flies*, is an execrable god who
delights in the whining self-abasement of his worshippers,
his senility being his one redeeming feature. Yet he is the

lord of the heavens and with the grand spectacle of cosmic order, presided over by the good, he tries to awe the Existentialist hero, Orestes, into submission. But in vain. The hero is unimpressed by the rhythm of rolling stars and fruit-bearing trees. In Aegisthus, adulterer, regicide, usurper, and tyrant, Jupiter finds a responsive partner:

> *Jupiter.* We have the same passion. You love order, Aegisthus.
> *Aegisthus.* Order—that is true. For the sake of order I seduced Clytemnestra; for the sake of order I killed my king. I wanted order to reign and to reign through me. I have lived without desire, love, and hope. But I have established order. O terrible and divine passion (II,3).

This is the Existentialist's choice: preferable to living under order is the flight into the desert with the furies on one's trail. For order is fraud and imposition. The world is truly a desert—a land without signs.

IV

Subjective Truth

IN AN ESTRANGED world information is available but no truth. "Truth about the world"—this mode of speech implies a meaningful or understandable whole, a cosmos. But the world is no longer recognized as cosmos, and by the same token truth as the revelation of meaning to man seems unattainable. If we call the organ of the revelation of meaning reason, then the experience of estrangement involves the eclipse of faith in reason. As the intelligible world is dismissed as a juvenile dream, the faculty of intellection, the inner eye for the vision of this world, continues, if at all, as a mere vestigial organ. In this sense Existentialism is a form of irrationalism, in spite of its professions of faith in science. In fact, neo-Positivism, that modern school of thought which makes it its business to glorify natural science as the only road to truth, is an unavowed nihilism and thereby akin to Existentialism. Talking about metaphysics (sign-reading in a world without signs), to them an impossible thing, the two schools use the same language, the neo-Positivists speaking with complacent tolerance—metaphysics, they say, is a sort of edifying poetry—the Existentialists with the accent of despair.

Plato, so Cicero tells us, was once stranded on a desolate shore. His companions took alarm, but Plato, noticing geometrical figures drawn in the sand, reassured them: he had discovered traces of humanity (*De re publica* i, 29). From the point of view of the experience of estrangement, Plato was too sanguine in his conclusion. Mathematics does not teach civilized behavior, and Plato and his companions might just as well have anticipated torture applied with scientific accuracy.

Truth as the disclosure of meaning is not to be wrested from the objects of the Existentialist's estranged world. If at all, it must be found in the inner man, as a condition or act of the mind. Instead of being objective, the essence of truth must lie in man's veracity or sincerity. To be in truth rather than to have truth will then be the goal to be striven after. Meaning, the Existentialist affirms, is not to be revealed as though it were available in a realm of essences. It must rather be brought into existence; it must be lived. And this living in truth is called emphatically existence. However, the subjective truth is not entirely severed from reference to things subsisting outside man. A negative reference persists. That no truth can be won from inspection of the world—this insight itself is a truth, and the introduction to truth in general. The revelation of meaninglessness is meaningful—and the foundation of all meaning. First we must run against the unyielding wall of an estranged world, then be sent back by rebound, as it were, into our inwardness. The redeeming answer must be discovered in the encounter with Nothingness.

No truth is available for an inspection of the world. The unavailability of objective truth in an estranged world can be expressed by the following disjunction:

I. Objective truth (that is, truth about . . .), by virtue

of its being known, becomes my, the knower's, truth and
thereby ceases to be truth.

II. My truth, by virtue of its being verified as objective
truth (that is, truth about . . .) ceases to be mine.

Putting the matter more briefly: truth cannot be my
truth, and my truth cannot be truth. The critical destruction of the idea of objective truth by means of this disjunction is carried out in Existentialist thought with the help
of two fundamental concepts: the idea of the concrete
individual and the idea of passion (or of man as a passionate being, an *animal passionale*).

I. *No objective truth can be my truth.* The correct understanding of this paradox depends on an adequate idea of
"mineness." The Existentialist may also be an idealist,
and both Heidegger and Sartre do come rather close to
being idealists. But they are not much troubled by the
old idealist puzzle, to wit: how my ideas, my thoughts, or
my perceptions as being in the mind can refer to existing
things outside the mind. This puzzle, according to Existentialist analysis, misses the real problem. It operates with
an abstract idea of the individual as mind in the sense of
the Cartesian *cogito*, as the subject of rational awareness.
Instead of the abstract self with its "I think," this concrete
self with its "I exist" or "I live" ought to be placed at
the beginning of philosophical reflection.

Man is not an absolute consciousness engrafted upon a
sentient organism and impeded, to some extent, by this
alliance with an unequal partner in its proper functioning.
Man is one, living and acting out of a center of spontaneity
within a concrete situation. "What really exists and counts
is this particular individual, the real individual which I
am, with the incredibly subtle structure of his experience,
with all the special features of the concrete adventure

which it is incumbent on him, and on him alone, to live out. How should all this be deduced?" (Gabriel Marcel, *Homo Viator*, pp. 190–91.) This concrete man is aware of this situation, forms ideas in regard to it, relates his appraisal of relevant data to his purposes and acts accordingly. But this awareness does not lift him out of the situation, transporting him, as it were, by a legerdemain from the dust and peril of the arena to a safe and lofty seat in the gallery. There is only an arena and no gallery. Thought, however high it may soar, remains elucidation of the situation which confines the thinking-living being. "Thought is unable to step out of existence" (*idem, Etre et avoir*, pp. 34–35). The physicist may well frame a theory which reduces time to the fourth dimension of a space-time continuum. Understanding and applying this theory, he must nonetheless relate it to the real world in which instruments are handled and real nails are driven into real boards with real hammers.

All our knowledge remains human, that is, bound up with a concrete situation within which we use things in the train of our vital preoccupations. Knowledge is orientation, by far the subtlest mode of dealing with a situation but still subject to the rules which determine the intercourse between the individual and his natural and human environment. Knowledge may consist in the possession of meaning. But a thing becomes meaningful precisely by taking its place within the vital context whose organizing principle is the "for the sake of . . ."— the subjective counterpart to the idea of the good (the "master sign" in a world really a world). At this juncture the Existentialist's affinity to American Pragmatism is evident.

The hammer is not first recognized as a lump of

material reality, located somewhere in space, and afterwards interpreted with reference to its purpose. We rather discover the hammer as the "thing with which to hammer." Our seeing the hammer is an anticipation of our handling it, and hammering with it is, so to speak, an activated acquaintance. What applies to this or any other tool is true of all things composing our world. The surface of the globe is discovered as the ground to stand on or the soil to cultivate, the sea as the boundary of the habitable continent or as the bridge linking one continent with another, the star as an "instrument of time," a plant as a vegetable or weed. In short, the character of the utensil is spread over the whole expanse of reality, stamping things with the human trade-mark of "utensility" (as *Zeug* or *das Zuhandene*, in Heidegger's untranslatable language). Accordingly, the mere "thingness" of things, their detached objectivity, far from being their natural status within human experience, is a modification of their original "usableness," a reduction of their functional concreteness to the neutral status of that which is "simply there" (*das Vorhandene*, in Heidegger)—to the status of *res*. It was the error of Descartes and his followers to consider the thing *qua res* the form under which reality normally reveals itself to human inspection (*Sein und Zeit*, pp. 63–113).

It is this their original "usableness" or serviceableness which, according to Heidegger's analysis, organizes things into what he calls "world." Its unity is provided by the unifying human concern under the form of the "for the sake of . . ." (*umwillen*), and this so organized whole, called "world," is familiar to us in advance of specific exploration. It is the "horizon" within which all discoveries are made. This so-called world, however, is a

totally different thing from the world as universe—from
that world which, by the Existentialist's hypothesis,
denies itself to man by its fundamental estrangement.
Heidegger's analyses presuppose the experience of estrangement and the denial of the cosmos. The possibility
of "signs" is ruled out tacitly and drastically. What is
left as "world" is merely the subjective correlate to the
sign-bearing cosmos, an *Ersatz* world—a world only in
the sense in which we speak of the "world of big business,"
the "world of the theater," or the "world of gamblers,"
but not world as cosmos. It is a world "projected" by
the self onto Nothingness and Nothingness shines through
the picture of the world as its ground. Its radical subjectivity is more obvious still in Sartre's simplified version
of Heidegger's "utensil-world."

Sarte, making extensive use of Hegel's dialectical
method and even his terminology, distinguishes between
the "in itself" (*l'en soi*) of objective Being and the "for
itself" (*le pour soi*) of the subject. The "for itself" is the
hole of nothingness amidst the density of Being. Speaking
with greater precision and using, at the same time, the
extraordinary language of Existentialism, we should call
the subject a "noughting nought" (*néant néantisant*)
which carves its world out of the block of Being by
means of negative determinations. This is Fichte in reverse. In Fichte the object is posited as non-ego. In
Sartre, the subject is a dynamic non-thing. In the light
of these principles we must understand Sartre's definition
of the world as a totality of utensils or rather as "the
undifferentiated ground against which there are discovered complexes indicative of 'utensility' " (*L'être et le
néant*, p. 252). "This totality of utensils," he writes, "is
the exact counterpart of my possibilities. And since I

am my possibilities, the order of utensils in the world is
the image, projected onto the 'in itself,' of my possibilities; that is to say, of what I am. But this mundane
image I am unable to decipher: I can only adapt myself
to it by action" (*ibid.*, p. 251).

While the world is, as it were, sucked into the ego
and transfigured into an enlarged self, the world as universe recedes beyond man's reach. It becomes in Sartre the
undifferentiated self-identity of the "in itself" of Being of
which nothing can be said except that it is, the ineffable
Sein in Heidegger, or the "Encompassing" (*das Umgreifende*) in Karl Jaspers' philosophy.

As Heidegger and Sartre are strongly influenced by
Hegel, so Jaspers is influenced by Kant. With him the
critique of our reasoning faculty plays a decisive role. Like
Kant's "thing in itself," the Encompassing in Jaspers recedes as human reason advances towards it—by its very
nature it is unapproachable and unthinkable. We perceive things, facts, complexes of facts, and in order to see
them correctly, we try to see them within the widest
relevant context; in other words, within their proper horizon. Then we proceed to take under observation this
wider context—only to discover that it in turn is circumscribed by a still wider horizon, and so forth. So the Encompassing is present to the mind only through negation
as the ever receding ground, unamenable to objectivity.
Any object, however comprehensive, is less than the Encompassing. For the Encompassing articulates itself into
three "regions" which it is impossible to enclose within
the limits of an object. One of these regions is Being as
the totality of being things (the Encompassing as object);
the second region is the Being that we are (the Encompassing as subject); the third is Reason which forms a bond

between the other two regions (*Von der Wahrheit* [1947], pp. 47–52).

This sounds very Hegelian, but the underlying view is rather remote from the spirit of Hegel's dialectic. What we are actually witnessing in Jaspers is the breaking asunder of the world (the world smitten by estrangement) into two components. One may be called the object-element —the Encompassing which withdraws as we try to grasp it. The other component (the subject-element) is a world picture, fully within our reach but actually nothing except our gesture of reaching, devoid of a definable reference to an independent object, an interpretation, in Jaspers' own words, without any underlying text (*ibid.*, p. 86). A tenuous link is left between the two halves, the unapproachable Being on the one hand and the Being as approach to nothing on the other. The latter, the world picture, is understood as a "perspective" on Being much in the same way in which Kant's phenomenal thing is supposed to be an appearance of the thing in itself. But the link, in the case of Jaspers, links something with nothing, the world picture (which is always the particular world picture of some particular person) with the negation of all particular world pictures. Thereby the world picture, without losing anything of its definiteness, becomes transparent towards Nothingness. It is no longer a picture of the world but a picture world—and there exists an indefinite number of them.

The attempt to replace the abstract subject of rationalist philosophy with the concrete individual ends in a curious paradox. This concrete individual, rather than living in the world, is his "world." This his world is like a halo which he radiates, an inseparable expression of his personality. "World" in this subjective sense is neither meaningless nor meaningful but it has just as much meaning as the individual succeeds in conferring upon it. "The world is human," Sartre writes (*op. cit.*, p. 270); in fact, so human that it ceases to be *the* world. It is an archaic world, or a Renaissance world, or an American world, or, in a final advance to undiluted particularity and concreteness, Alexander's world, my world, someone's world. In the absence of the world, worlds multiply. Heraclitus remarked scornfully that men behaved as though they lived each in his separate world (Diels, *Fragmente der Vorsokratiker* [5th ed., 1934], I, 151, fr. 2). And they so live because they must, the Existentialist retorts.

Through becoming my truth, truth ceases to be true. The significance which accrues to the possessive pronoun from the preceding reflections makes this paradox plausible or at least meaningful. For to become mine means for truth as well as for anything else to become absorbed into that unique and unitary whole which is the concrete individual. Normally, truth is truth about something for someone. Now this latter relationship (true for someone) swallows, so to speak, the reference to the object. Of course, some reference to objects will have to persist, lest communication break down completely. So theology will continue to be about God, astronomy about stars, sociology about social life. But this objective reference is given significance only by the dominant relation to the subject for which these objects exist: God will be "God such as I experience him"; the heavens will be the heavens as interpreted by the Greeks or the age of the relativity theory; society will be society as conceived by Jeffersonian Liberalism, and so forth. How then can truth, being mine, still be truth? In order to verify an idea or theorem I must test its adequacy to the object on which it bears. But I, being a concrete individual myself, have no access to the object as such. I have only my view of it. The idea of the concrete individual proves destructive of objective truth.

The concrete individual, far from being a static entity, is life, a process, a continual flux. It is not only temporal in the sense in which the phenomenal world and all its parts are temporal. Its very nature is temporality. The individual exists only in the living present, the concrete moment "now," and past and future, rather than being external to this present moment, are enclosed within it, the past as time recollected, the future as time anticipated. To live for the individual means to be present and yet to live outside this present moment in his own past and his own future, with things past and with things future. Making the utmost of etymology, Heidegger throws this feature of the self into prominence by writing "ek-sistence" and by calling man an "ec-static" being, and Sartre follows suit. Being a self means to be outside oneself, on the flight from oneself, and the "world" which every individual claims for himself is the encrustation of this centrifugal move; it is human temporality, Time proper, crystallized into that rectilinear sequence of events which characterizes physical time. This, at any rate, is the view presented by Heidegger for whom man is essentially a "centrifugal being"—*ein Wesen der Ferne* (*Vom Wesen des Grundes*, p. 40). According to Sartre, the self is flight in a different sense. The Now in which the self has its being, with its headlong rush down the steep decline of receding past, he interprets as the flight of the "for itself" (*le pour soi*) from the "in itself" (*l'en soi*) which is brought to an end by death, the final triumph of the "in itself" (*op. cit.*, p. 193).

Truth is functionalized through appropriation by the concrete individual. By the same token it is temporalized.

It is made out to be something that happens. But truth cannot be described as happening unless it ceases to be truth about something. The truth that "fastens" must yield to all-powerful process. This unrestricted prevalence of process over static being is the one feature which Heidegger and Sartre share with Whitehead. At their hands even language, the vehicle of truth, must submit to forceful temporalization. Most of their neologisms consist in the transformation of nouns into *Zeitwörter* (verbs, literally "time-words"). Heidegger, for example, has *nichten, welten, anwesen* (to nought, to world, to presentify itself), and Sartre follows him with *néantiser, possibiliser, présentifier* (to nought, to possible, to presentify), and the like.

As truth is made subjective and thereby temporal, philosophy becomes historiography of the human mind. This idea, foreshadowed in Hegel, is given a radical expression by Heidegger: he hopes to uncover with his analyses the hidden *Urgeschichte* (primal history) of man (*Vom Wesen des Grundes*, p. 28). The point of view according to which all knowledge must be interpreted in terms of history is historicism, and Existentialism may be called historicism grown desperate. Heidegger's claim to carry Wilhelm Dilthey's thought to its logical conclusions is by no means void.

One of the inescapable implications of historicism is the destruction of the meaning of history. History is meaningful only through reference of the temporal process to a supratemporal scheme of interpretation. But if the scheme of interpretation is itself in process, history ceases to be intelligible. It becomes pulverized into a sequence of moments, each of which can reflect all others (or at least all preceding ones), but only in the manner in which Leibniz's windowless monads reflect each other: no real interaction takes place. There is no mathematics, but there is a Greek mathematics and a Baroque mathematics, just as there are many architectures: Hellenic, Baroque, and numerous others. The persistence of general classes and types under such titles as "the science of mathematics" or "the art of building" seems of little account. What matters is the temporal act of creation—the *Weltanschauung* or *Zeitgeist*—which at a given moment animates and organizes all works of the mind—mathematical theorems, buildings, musical compositions, astronomical discoveries, deeds of statecraft, forms of worship, philosophical systems —into one unique whole, the Baroque world or Goethe's world, or the world of Mr. X.

Dilthey tried to escape the absurdity of it all—mirrors mirroring mirrors which mirror the void—by classifying those fundamental creative conceptions, called *Weltanschauungen*, under types. But no typology will liberate the concrete individual from his captivity in the moment. It succeeds merely in adding the "typological world view" as a fresh variety to the vast array of *Weltanschauungen*. The only link between the monadic moments, simulating rather than providing continuity, is the abstract idea of flux. Life, then, presents itself as an amorphous stream out of which forms crystallize incessantly—cultures, societies, and their institutions and works. But it is only for a moment that they sparkle in the light. A minute later the stream, a destructive as well as a creative power, will have carried them away. This view of things, generally identified as "philosophy of life" (*Lebensphilosophie*), is the elegiac anticipation of Existentialism proper.

The nemesis of the dissolution of history into an amorphous life stream is the emergence of fate, a senseless necessity. Oswald Spengler's *Decline of the West* (1918) made so deep an impression because it combined the three characteristic features of historicist disintegration (the pluralism of self-enclosed moments, the elegiac view of the transience of forms, and fatalism) into a logically brittle but imaginatively powerful whole. An Existentialist like Jaspers, reflecting on the concrete individual, notices that "we" (he likes to speak in the name of all of us, as spokesman of the *Zeitgeist*) are not like other people in the past. They, the people of the past, did not suffer from historicist scruples. They were "naïve." They spoke, for example, of God, and they did not reflect that this was just "the God of the men of the Age of Enlightenment." Or they spoke of virtues and vices, and it did not occur to them that they expressed just the scale of values peculiar to the feudal society of Christian Europe. They were not unaware of the limitations of human knowledge in general and theirs in particular and, prudent men that they were, they made allowance for the possibility of error. But they were convinced that they were dealing with realities and enunciating, in their own blundering way, "the things that are." They had not yet, the Existentialist believes, discovered the concrete individual and the primacy of time, nor, consequently, the full scope of human freedom. How explain this late arrival of bitter knowledge?

With the answer to this question the idea of fate is urged upon the mind. These men of the past, the answer reads, were living under the tutorship of publicly recognized and effective traditions in religion, metaphysics, and social and political life. As a result, they found it easy to understand each other and to interpret, or rather misinterpret, the publicly acknowledged views as those which revealed reality. The course of events which

led from the Middle Ages through Renaissance, Enlightenment, and Romanticism to this present age is to
be interpreted as the gradual destruction of traditional
shelters and barriers, the progress towards catastrophe,
the emancipation of man from kindly illusions, and his
issuing forth into his terrible freedom.

Man must be uprooted in order to understand what
the Existentialist teaches. He must be, like Sartre's
Orestes, a man "freed from all servitudes and beliefs,
without a family, a country, or a religion," free like a
gossamer thread (*The Flies*, I, 2). Yet the Existentialist
who prides himself on his disillusionment has his own
kind of naïveté. No doctrinaire of the eighteenth century
could have been more dogmatic in placing himself and
his time at the culminating point of the historical curve
than Jaspers is in determining our place at the absolute
nadir (*Die geistige Situation der Zeit*, Berlin, Leipzig, 1931).
He sees estrangement closing down upon us with in-
exorable necessity, and Existentialism is for him the
awareness of the completion of this process and, thereby,
the unprecedented disclosure of man's actual situation—
his mortal affliction and his great chance.

Every step in the progress towards estrangement has
for Jaspers the sanctity of a decree of fate. Nietzsche came
—"the greatest intellectual event in recent history"—and
said, "God is dead." From that time on, Jaspers suggests,
God has been actually dead in a very real sense. Once
God is equated with God-consciousness, a man may be
said to "slay" God, and this was done by Nietzsche. It is
no longer possible to believe in God after Nietzsche in
the same way in which it was possible to believe in him
before the event, Jaspers holds. Hegel himself could not
have shown more deference towards history than the

Existentialist here does. This is the reverse side of the disintegration of history into monadic moments: as the de-
terminant of our situation, history takes on the aspect of
a demonic power, which forces us into the presence of a
spiritual void. The encounter with Nothingness is made
to appear the fate of our time.

The historical moment does not have the coercive
power which the Existentialist tends to ascribe to it, and
it is a hazardous thing to speak of "our time" as a uniform and universally shared condition. With these reser-
vations in mind we shall find the Existentialist diagnosis
of the contemporary world sufficiently accurate to dispel
complacency. Jaspers writes:

> The physiognomy of our age is determined through-
> out by the *unsheltered man*, be he revealed in the rebel-
> lion of defiance, or in the despair of nihilism, or in the
> helplessness of the many frustrated people, or finally in
> the erring quest of those who scorn the safety offered
> by finite knowledge and resist the enticement of com-
> fortably harmonious solutions. There is no God, the
> swelling masses clamor. As a result man becomes
> worthless; he can be slaughtered in any numbers,
> because he is nothing (p. 130).

Historicism applied to practice proves ambiguous. It
provides neither a program of action nor guiding principles, but it tends to encourage one or the other of two
extreme attitudes, quietism or activism. If there are no
timeless principles, if every situation, every civilization
and people, every individual develops in accordance with
its unique entelechy, then the individual has no legitimate
ground for taking sides, fighting the evil and taking a firm

stand in defense of what he considers right. He must let history "grow." This apparently is the philosophy of the frogs in Aesop's fable. Zeus, seeing how these gentle animals are disposed, will not fail to send them a truly active ruler, not sharing but utilizing their philosophy: a stork.

Sartre shows us how the Existentialist premises may lead to the diametrically opposed conclusion of activism. Since history provides no principles of action, he argues, the acting individual must invent his own principles and then do accordingly. During the occupation a young man sought M. Sartre's advice: Should he stay with his helpless mother or go abroad to join the *Forces Françaises Libres?* Moral philosophers ever since Aristotle have taught that there is no such thing as theoretical casuistry. This is to say that the subsumption of a particular situation under a rule of conduct is not to be expected from theory but requires in addition to theory a combination of wisdom and tact. But Sartre, taking advantage of this limitation of moral philosophy, jumped to the conclusion that universal principles of conduct are simply nonexistent. His advice was accordingly: Do what you please but do it wholeheartedly and imaginatively. Invent the person you are to be and stick to your invention (*L'existentialisme, etc.*, pp. 39–49). A similar activism animated the sophisticated youth of Italy in giving support to Fascism. They were not so naïve as to accept at its face value the Duce's melodramatic story of a resurrection of Eternal Rome. But they thought it worthier, or perhaps only more exciting, to do something spectacular now than to wait for timeless verities to give them employment. If truth is not available, why not make the most of the semblance within our reach?

The concrete individual grows so concrete that it tolerates no concreteness beside itself. The idea that objective truth, by becoming my (the concrete individual's) truth, ceases to be truth, appears no longer as a playful paradox. We now turn to the other side of the picture.

II. *No truth which is mine can be an objective truth.* In order to understand this second paradox, we must remember that the individual, aside from being concrete in the just defined sense, is also endowed with passion. From his passionate nature a meaning accrues to the possessive pronoun which still remains to be explored. There is an accent of gravity in our saying, my body, my house, my child, my knowledge, my God, which we must be careful to discern. We must distinguish degrees of belonging, and our paradox apparently suggests that the most intimate appropriation excludes the objectivity of demonstrable truth. And passion may be that power which totally incorporates its object into the ego. Most emphatically mine is that to which I cling passionately, that is, at any cost. If this "at any cost" is taken strictly as it should be taken, the number of things emphatically mine shrinks almost to nil. We do not cling to life at any cost, for we are willing to lay it down in the service of our country. And again we are willing to give up our country if faith and honor require us to do so. We begin to see that passion differs from emotional attachment by degree of intensity, but so that the difference of degree amounts to a difference of kind. In the light of these explanations we may rephrase our paradox as follows: "No truth which is mine in the sense of being the basis of my existence can be an objective truth."

An astronomer makes observations on the rings of Saturn, and after he has published his results, they become common property of scientists in the field. In a restricted sense, this bit of empirical knowledge was originally the astronomer's knowledge, yet that fact in no wise militates against its objective status as a contribution to astronomy.

One in a group of shipwrecked people who have been afloat in a lifeboat for several days and whose provisions begin to run low, discovers at the horizon a rapidly approaching ship. He will not coolly take note of this fact but his whole heart will go out to the ship of salvation and the thrill of delight will pierce him with painful vehemence. The discovery will become at once an integral part of his life and, in fact, of his personality. To the end of his days, he will remain the one who once believed he was lost until he discovered a streak of smoke, a promise of life in his agony.

Although in the second case the discovery is much more intimately belonging to the discoverer than is true of the astronomical observation, the objective validity and verifiability of the truth discovered continue important elements in the situation. In fact, they are all the more important because of the vital interest attached to the object. The anguish of the man in peril of life sharpens his eyes while at the same time blunting his critical judgment. So his chance to discover truth will be both better and worse than that of the detached astronomer.

The man scanning the horizon in anguish and espying at last what he longs for, discovers not some alien thing merely, an unknown ship, but himself, his survival, his life. This is why the sight takes lodging at once in the core of his self. For the very being of the self consists in being concerned about itself. As an individual I *am*, in the specific sense that this being of mine is a matter of dominant interest for me. To live means for the individual: to be and to will his being, the two aspects forming an inseparable unity. The peculiar structure of the subjective "world," so our earlier analysis has shown, is determined by concern under the form of the "for the sake of. . . ." This teleological structure, as we now come to see, has its origin in that ultimate interest for the sake of which other ends are pursued and with a view to which our "utensil-world" is organized.

Let us suppose for a moment that this concern for ourselves were exhausted by concern for physical survival and that consequently the situation of the shipwrecked party were symbolic of life in general. In that case, objective truth about certain facts would be of ultimate significance. The word of the physician would announce to the patient salvation or perdition, and the scientist would take the place of the priest. In these conditions life would become a different thing from what we know it to be. This is not to say that it would be comparable in terrors to the existence in a boat adrift on the ocean. For the terrors of the sea would be less terrible if the shipwrecked voyager's concern were solely with the preservation of his life. All that can be said about this imaginary type of life is that it would be infinitely drearier than actual life, poorer in both fears and hopes.

The Existentialist, in defining selfhood as infinite concern about one's own being, does not have so distorted and base a conception of life as to identify this fundamental self-will with the will to survival. The basic will or concern may involve a will to life, even to eternal life, but not as simple perpetuity which might be prolonged misery and tedium. We, the non-Existentialists, would say that this will's aim is God, and that this involves our life with God. But the Existentialist, of course, will not agree. He must refrain from assigning to the fundamental concern a definable goal, for his assertion that "true" or "authentic" existence is aimed at can hardly be regarded as an acceptable definition, authenticity or sincerity being among the achievements which cannot be striven after directly. But this much is clear: in the concern under consideration, there is fused the insatiable avidity for life and self-perpetuation with the insistence of the moral imperative. Understood in this manner the idea of "concern" or "care" is no newcomer to the history of philosophy. Socrates in Plato's *Apology* exhorts his fellow citizens to care for "themselves" rather than for what is merely theirs, to care for the "city itself" rather than merely for its appurtenances, and so in everything else (36 c, d). As we associate the "care" in the *Apology* with the idea of love (*eros*) in the *Banquet*, we come very close to the concept of self-concern which is here relevant.

Being concerned about himself is for the individual the theme of his life, constituting him as an ego. And this concern is infinite or absolute, that is to say, it takes precedence over all other concerns, desires, or interests. An absolute concern or interest we call passion. Whatever else is referred to as a passion, the passion of the lover or the artist or the gambler, must then derive its intensity from man's primary passion. Both by their sublimity and destructive ferocity those passions reveal man's inmost nature, that insistence on the absolute which stamps him as the *animal passionale*.

If passionate self-concern is of the essence of selfhood, the things which belong to the self in a more than accidental fashion and which are emphatically mine will be those which are seized upon and assimilated by that fundamental drive. Applying this to knowledge, we remember our earlier formula: "No truth which is mine in the sense of being the basis of my existence can be an objective truth." And this is so, we may now add by way of explanation, because man is passionately concerned about the basis of his existence. At this juncture the assertion that the intimacy of its belonging to me, its being entirely mine, excludes objectivity of truth begins to look plausible. We descry the limitations of the analogy of the man in the lifeboat. In one sense the analogy is revealing. Like one in deadly peril, we scan the horizon for a sign of salvation. In another sense the analogy misleads. For to think of this "sign of salvation" in terms of an objective fact, ascertainable by science, gets us involved in absurdities.

A few years ago a distinguished scientist traveled up and down the country, bringing to college audiences the glad tidings of man's freedom as certified by modern physics. His argument had been advanced before, mostly by physicists, refuted before, mostly by philosophers, and it is still being reiterated as though it might gain force by dint of repetition. It is maintained that, while classic physics taught strict determinism to the exclusion of freedom, modern physics, thanks to Heisenberg's indeterminacy factor, restores the idea of freedom to intellectual respectability. The point of the argument is, of course, that the existence of freedom as well as our awareness of it is of fundamental value to man and that we owe deep gratitude to nuclear physicists for what they have done for us in our capacity as moral beings.

We who consider the argument fallacious refuse to acknowledge that particular debt. But we should go further and make it clear that, if the argument were correct, we would have to regard scientists as dangerous people rather than as benefactors. For two hundred years, so we should then argue, they denied man's dignity, and they did so on good though not on sufficient grounds. Now, as a by-product of atomic research, they return to us the permission to conceive of ourselves as free and responsible agents. But for how long? What entitles us to think of quantum mechanics as a final accomplishment rather than as a phase in the unfinished development of physics? Shall the children of this age stand in breathless expectancy before the closed doors of the laboratory (no admittance for laymen!), waiting for the word to come from the lips of the academically approved hierophant—the word that reveals to them the truth (for the time being) about themselves?

Obviously the presuppositions of the argument are perversely wrong. Man may be miserable. But his misery is not adequately illustrated by the castaway's plight. The latter's fate depends on the message of his eyes. The objective reality, ascertainable only by actual experience, of what he thinks he sees spells life or death to him. But there is, to say the least, something improbable or even shocking in the idea that the decision regarding man's nature—a question on which our spiritual welfare hinges—should be equally dependent on verification through empirical science. By admitting this dependence we would place man's destiny at the mercy of the vicissitudes and aberrations to which science is subject. We would thereby imperil life which needs for its guidance principles of more than hypothetical validity; and we would corrupt science which needs for its free development a grand unconcern about the immediate practical consequences of its theorems.

Science, however, is not the only steward of objective truth and, to make good his contention, the Existentialist must carry his attack further. He must try to show that metaphysics is as incapable as science of providing truths of ultimate significance, that is, truths which by their nature demand to be embraced with passion as emphatically mine. If he should be successful in proving his point, he would set an end to metaphysics. Precisely this Kierkegaard hopes to achieve by having recourse to a "reduction to absurdity" not unlike the one used by us here in dealing with science.

Suppose a *Privatdozent* (that peculiar chrysalis which is to develop into a professor of philosophy) teaches a course in metaphysics. He is, so Kierkegaard assumes as a matter of course, a Hegelian, and he will unfold, neatly divided into sections, subsections, and paragraphs, the system of the world as planned by Supreme Reason. In the concluding subsection on the "absolute life of the Spirit," the purpose and meaning of that grand spectacle, the universe, after long and laborious preparations, will finally be revealed to his hearers. Suppose now that one of his students is prevented from attending the closing lectures. Then the clue to life is withheld from him and his academic irregularity may cost him his eternal salvation. But this apparently is preposterous. Should we actually allow demonstrations—or the absence of them—to be our upbuilding or undoing? Are we not making a demand on reason which reason is unable to fulfill? Are we not, in making this demand, in the sorry position of one who desires to become a lover but first requires conclusive proof of the worthiness of the one to be loved?

Behind these jests and rhetorical appeals there hides a real dilemma. Meaning is discovered by the student of objects only through seeing these objects as forming a whole—a universe. But to see the universe as a whole implies looking at it as though he, the beholder, were placed outside or above the universe. The speculative philosopher arrogates to himself God's own perspective. But the passionate interest with which the concrete individual searches for *his* truth, *his* meaning, as a foundation upon which to build his life, is bound up with his finitude. The human quest is prompted by the heat, confusion, and mortal anguish of one struggling in the melee, not by the detached interest of the umpire whose seat lifts him high above the struggle. Even if we grant to the metaphysician that he has actually achieved what he says is his purpose and if we accept his system as a faithful rendition of reality, his account would yet be utterly useless to us. "Wonderful," we would say to him, "your achievement deserves to be awarded a prize by the National Academy. Unfortunately, however, we have not yet attained to the condition of disembodied spirits; we are still engaged in the business of living our lives. As a pastime we find your system both entertaining and stimulating, and we shall not fail to include it in our new curriculum by which we hope to revolutionize the humanities program. But surely you do not expect us to take it seriously?" Objective truth reveals itself to the detached spectator. Vital truth is grasped with the passionate anxiety of a drowning man grabbing the life belt. Should these two things go together? Never, the Existentialist avers. Vital truth is truth in time, for me, the real person. Speculative truth is eternal truth, out of touch with time, and reaching it means to get away from one's self.

Trying to make as strong a case for the Existentialist as we can and disregarding the misgivings we feel (we are concocting an intellectual poison in defaming reason), we may essay the following experiment. Let us imagine ourselves as citizens of Plato's ideal republic. In this community nothing is more strictly guarded against than the idea that any good deed might go unrewarded or that the evildoer might thrive. Both the universe and the state so clearly exhibit all-powerful justice that no room is left for moral doubt or metaphysical scruples. Shall we, placed in this artificial environment, continue to be moral agents? This is seriously to be doubted. Wrongdoing, in these conditions, would be rank folly; virtue, a matter of cleverness and a little self-control. But that means that right and wrong would no longer be what they now are. The righteousness of the mis-judged sufferer would seem the invention of blasphemous fancy, and there would be no greater thing in life than conformity. Our experiment confronts us with the pic-ture of a dull and loathsome life. But such would be our real life, the Existentialist argues, if objective truth (truth about the world) could be our truth.

Truth, Kierkegaard concludes, is subjective. It lies in the attitude of the individual towards an object, not in the object revealing itself to the individual. He writes:

> When the question of truth is raised in an objective manner, reflection is directed objectively to the truth. . . . If only the object to which he is related is the truth, the subject is accounted to be in the truth.

This is the view Kierkegaard rejects. He continues:

> When the question of the truth is raised subjectively, reflection is directed subjectively to the nature of the individual's relationship; if only the mode of this rela-tionship is in the truth, the individual is in the truth even if he should happen to be thus related to what is not true.

To bear out his contention Kierkegaard uses this illustration:

> If one goes up to the house of the true God, with the true conception of God in his knowledge, and prays, but prays in a false spirit; and one who lives in an idolatrous community prays with the entire passion of the infinite, although his eyes rest upon the image of an idol: Where is there most truth? The one prays in truth to God, though he worships an idol; the other prays falsely to the true God, and hence worships in fact an idol (*Concluding Unscientific Postscript* [Princeton, 1944], pp. 178–80).

If everything depends on how a truth is held, with what passionate zeal, while the reference to an object is of little or no account, strange consequences result. We have heard people praised for their sincerity and passionate devotion in adhering to National Socialism or Communism. Are they right because they are sincere? Is their faith true because they cling to it with fanatical zeal? Or is not rather their passionate devotion indicative of the degree to which their minds are enmeshed in error?

It is time for us to separate the wheat from the chaff in the argument which concludes from the concrete and impassioned individual upon the subjectivity of truth.

V

Gravediggers at Work

WE THINK OF the so-called analysts or semanticists as experts in the art of "debunking." You say "God," and they ask you: What do you mean by God? You say "freedom," and they ask: What do you mean by freedom? You try to explain, but they find your explanations unsatisfactory. "Rhetoric," is their verdict, and they conclude that you like others are using meaningless words.

The analysts perform their cure with an acid, burning away cankerous growths and, occasionally, also the live organs. The Existentialists form a much more ruthless demolition squad. They do have some understanding of the great words, yet by means of a slight but fatal omission they turn wholesome ideas into instruments of destruction. They are not concerned with the Nothingness in language only but with Nothingness as such. They purport not merely to purify our speech but to purge our souls at the risk of killing them in the process. Instead of an acid they use, so to speak, nuclear fission.

The Existentialist's emphasis on the concrete individual animated by passionate concern rescues from forgetfulness an important truth about man. But he mars his discovery by overlooking or rejecting three metaphysical concepts which alone could make it fruitful: the idea of contemplation, the idea of love, and the idea of rational faith.

The Existentialist deserves praise for repudiating the rationalist construction of man as a "thinking thing" (*res cogitans*) and recalling to us that concrete whole which every one of us is: not reason engrafted upon animality, but a living being whose vitality flowers into spiritual life; not just the specimen of the genus *homo sapiens*, but a unique individual, the son of his time and people, nourished and fashioned by the world which surrounds him; not knowing and in addition acting, but living in intelligent awareness of himself and the world. Knowledge, Heidegger rightly affirms, is "a mode of man's being in the world" (*Sein und Zeit*, p. 61). It has "existential" significance. All this is true and important to remember. But at once the deviation begins. The encounter with Nothingness casts its shadow on the analysis.

The human counterpart to being, the existential mode of our apprehending it, is contemplation. Ontology, the theory of being as a constructive principle, requires an existential supplement: the idea of life reaching its consummation in an act of vision. This dual conception— being linked with *vita contemplativa*—was framed in Greece by Parmenides and Plato. It was not abandoned but modified and deepened by Christian thinkers. For the Christian, too, beatitude, the supernatural acme of life, is vision, but vision of God who is the Being of all being things, though He is more than this—infinitely more. Accordingly, vision of God even at its highest must not be conceived as the full presence of God to the soul, but rather as the fullest visualization of His inscrutability. The

"face to face" is predicated upon a disposition of the will
to unfailing obedience towards God and loving fellowship
towards others. But whether we consider contemplative
life in its terrestrial approximation or its transterrestrial
perfection—in no case does it contradict or exclude the
idea of the concrete individual. It rather presupposes it.
It is the concrete individual attaining to his full stature.

The human counterpart to non-Being or Nothingness,
the existential mode of our apprehending it, is a counter-
feit contemplation—contemplation emptied of its original
plenitude of meaning. As Heidegger describes *theoria*, the
pure act of intellectual sight, it is in fact an existential
mode, but one defined by negations. It is misinterpreted
as a gaping or staring at objects, that is to say, as a "pri-
vative mode" of behavior compared with the vital circum-
spection guided by concern which generally enlightens
man about himself and the world. Heidegger, in this
connection, quotes St. Augustine's passages on curiosity
(*Confessions*, X, 35) while withholding their real meaning.
St. Augustine is interested in making a fundamental distinction between thirst for knowledge (which is God-
directed) and curiosity. For Heidegger no such difference
exists (*Sein und Zeit*, pp. 170–73).

In repudiating the Hellenic-Christian idea of contemplation along with its object and replacing it with a sorry
substitute, the Existentialist completes a process of disintegration that has been going on for several centuries.
It begins with the "Philosophy of the Moderns" in the
seventeenth century. With Descartes' construction of mind
as a "thinking thing," the existential significance of contemplation, its power of transforming the whole man and
assimilating him to the object, is blurred though not yet
obliterated.

Grown effete at the hands of Empiricists and Rationalists alike, contemplation is then formally denied its traditional place by Kant. Under the influence of Rousseau, according to his own confession, he emancipates himself from the belief that it is advance in knowledge (*theoria*) which constitutes "the honor of humanity" (Vorländer's edition, VIII, 273 ff.). Schopenhauer seems to reclaim the lost property of metaphysics but actually ruins it by assigning to intellectual intuition a novel object: blind, irrational will, an anticipation of the Existentialist's active Nothing. With him the bliss of vision is sheer negation, a deliverance from the toil of life, the deep draught of Nothingness. Love in morbid ecstasy turns to destruction, and the road lies open for nineteenth-century nihilism.

Nietzsche inherits Schopenhauer's negative concept of contemplation—and rejects it as a phenomenon of decadence. The idea of both a contemplative life and the will to truth which animates it is convicted as a refined expression of Platonic-Christian hostility towards life. With Nietzsche it becomes clear that the repudiation of the *vita contemplativa* involves a breaking away from the intellectual tradition which begins with Plato and is identical with the history of Hellenic-Western philosophy—even its adversaries depend upon it by virtue of their opposition. Heidegger, in a recent publication, draws the inevitable conclusion. According to him the great deviation, though a creative one, started with Plato, and its name is philosophy. It has now run its course and a new truth is dawning over the débris of our shattered civilization (*Platons Lehre von der Wahrheit*, Bern, 1947).

The sublimity of indifferent knowledge, tested by Christian seriousness, stands revealed as jesting and vanity, Kierkegaard affirms (*Sickness unto Death*, Preface). This facile equation of contemplation with "indifferent knowledge" shows to what extent the authentic idea of vision is alien from Kierkegaard's mind. That sight might be the fruit of a love which has gone through its worst crisis—this idea does not occur to him, and St. Augustine's teaching on Christian Wisdom finds no echo in his thinking. He sees only the infinite contrast that exists between the finite human perspective on the one hand and God's infinite and all-comprehensive vision on the other. It is, we shall admit, good and wholesome to bear in mind and feel incessantly that tension, even to the point of acute distress and anguish over our remoteness from truth. But it is equally important to remember the possibility of mediation between these poles which Kierkegaard, with his debilitated idea of contemplation, holds in scorn. True, we are unable ever to bridge the gulf between our creaturely selves and God, the "wholly other," by our own effort—we need to be carried across it. Yet, as truly as contemplative life is a reality, there is also that existential growth towards vision which we call ascent: the transforming rise towards a more comprehensive though still limited perspective, the human counterpart to the analogical structure of reality which in all its remoteness from God yet bears testimony to Him as its maker. Kierkegaard, in discarding the contemplative life, must also dismiss ascent as an illusion or worse, as a blasphemous attempt to debase God's truth into a human possession. The surrender of the idea of ascent involves the cancellation of *paideia*, the Platonic concept of education, and the old adage that "truth will make you free" is no longer recognized. The story referred to in the preceding chapter—about the student of metaphysics cutting the concluding lectures and thereby missing the point in both the system and his life—this story is funny and its moral is plausible only to one who considers Plato's report on the steep and laborious ascent from the cave to the upper world an arrogant fancy rather than a truth-telling myth.

For obvious reasons the abandonment of contemplation and ascent must be fatal to truth. It is the fundamental thesis of Reinhold Niebuhr's theology that man's relation to history is ambiguous. While being immersed in the historical flux, he yet transcends it. Accepting this view as correct, we add that ascent culminating in vision is the transcending move under the aspect of the intellect. To deny ascent is to deny the possibility of transcendence with the result that the individual as an intelligent being becomes entirely submerged in the moving patterns of history. The vantage point above the flux and even the possibility of an approximation to it vanish, and knowledge, functionalized, becomes an expression of the fleeting moment. Philosophy finds itself irretrievably caught in the historicist plight.

The other Existentialist motif, passion as the fundamental trait of the concrete individual, similarly combines an important insight with a fatal omission. Under the impression of technical progress, relative political stability, and positivistic thought, the conception of man as a gentle animal developed into a popular myth. Violence in human behavior, so the uncodified creed of this complacent modernism reads, is a relic of an earlier barbarous stage of evolution. It will be sloughed off gradually as mankind advances towards higher forms of technological development and social organization. Man will become more enlightened. He will learn to strive only after things within his reach, tempering the heat of his desire by the reflection that the welfare of the community is also the individual's welfare. In so becoming civilized, man will leave behind religion in its traditional form. For religion with its appeal to an ultimate hope and an ultimate fear keeps alive that intemperance of aspiration which is the mother of fanaticism and its sinister attendants: intolerance, persecution, tyranny, and war.

In attacking this secularist credo, the Existentialist rightly affirms that passion is of the essence of man. The champions of the "gentle animal" purge away the humanity of man along with his fierceness. That same passionate intensity which as insane fury drives nation against nation in internecine warfare is also responsible for all the great things man has ever achieved—his discoveries and peaceful conquests; his works of technical skill, fine art, and statecraft; his acts finally of devotion, self-sacrifice, and saintliness. Not by stifling the deep urge of man can he become civilized but only by releasing that passionate devotion which is creative of order rather than antagonistic to it. "Man does not live by bread alone." Bread may stand here for all the goods which are either necessary for the sustenance of life or desirable as amenities of life—that is to say, things which are normally pursued with great eagerness but which may also be thrown away for the sake of something greater. They are goods which by themselves do not enlist passion, although passion may take them as a pretext. Economic expansion and better living conditions, for example, serve nationalists as a pretext for venting the passionate desire for self-aggrandizement.

"Man does not live by bread alone." The Grand Inquisitor in Dostoyevsky's *Brothers Karamazov* quarrels with the Christian interpretation of this dictum because it overrates the common man's willingness to make sacrifices. But this much the great cynic admits: Man will rather not live than live a life without a meaning, that is, without an object of absolute or passionate devotion. The events of our time bear out the Grand Inquisitor. Wherever democracy is understood to offer nothing better than freedom in the sense of *laissez faire* and economic betterment, it is defeated by modern dictatorship which, whether Fascist or Communist, is politically organized fanaticism. For man, as revealed by his collective action, is neither wise nor mean. Once he is roused to decisive action, he will prefer a great wickedness to a petty goodness. This is why the interpretations of National Socialism by American secularists, as, for example, by John Steinbeck in *The Moon is Down*, are sorely inadequate. The humble people whom Steinbeck opposes to the proud militarists are precisely those who fall an easy prey to the dictatorial lure.

Once more the great and timely truth which the Existentialist proclaims is marred by an oversight. The concept of passion defined in terms of absolute intensity and detached from an object deprives him of the possibility of distinguishing between good passion and evil passion, between the divine and the demonic. "Love the Lord thy God with all thy heart, and with all thy soul, and with all thy mind." This demand, terrifying though it is, because only a saint truly satisfies it, yet expresses the philosophically correct idea of passion by assigning to it its proper object. Only by this addition of an object, unacceptable, of course, under the dispensation of Nothingness, does it become possible to distinguish the idolatrous passion of nationalism (the contemporary manifestation of pride or self-worship) from authentic devotion and to win a criterion by which to determine how things and persons should be humanly loved. It is, finally, the conjunction of love with contemplation and ascent which saves *theoria* from that negative interpretation ("the sublimity of indifferent knowledge") which sets a division between intellect and will.

Love is passion that has come into its own, and the proper object of love, God, as the First Love, the *summum amabile*, is also the regulating and guiding principle of theoretical life—the assurance that the intellectual quest leads to something worth knowing. Unless passion, through assignment to it of the proper object, is enabled to direct the aspiration of knowledge toward its natural goal, one of two things will happen to *theoria*, both equally calamitous. First, it will find itself confronted with Nothingness, the total vacuity of meaning, which is thrown into relief rather than mitigated by the vestiges of order and regularity that science discovers among existing things. The myth of the "Veiled Image at Sais," in Schiller's poem, will then be a telling symbol of the philosophical enterprise: unveiled, the Image brings death to the beholder.

This first conclusion regarding the meaning of *theoria* will readily lead to another one. Vision, after all, is a part of life. What can prompt the individual to offer himself to destruction? What is the spring behind his suicidal curiosity? There is such a thing, the answer reads, as the enticement of the abyss. There is a voluptuousness of destruction and a love (we use this word with hesitation) of Nothingness. That the lure of the depth is of intoxicating sweetness, bearing as it does a treacherous resemblance to the true nostalgia of the soul, the Romantic poets have shown us. The Blessed Damozel has a family likeness to Lamia, and the fine poison of nihilism is mixed into the liquid melodies of the "Hymns to the Night" and the

Tristan music. Nietzsche (hating Wagner because he gives away the secret also of his, Nietzsche's, soul) draws the inevitable conclusion. The thirst for knowledge, he holds, is the disease of a will perversely desirous of its own undoing, and in the scholar's will to truth Christian asceticism survives with its hankering after self-mortification. This is more than the emasculation of the contemplative ideal. It is its demonic counterpart—vision not as the light and consummation of love, but as the weapon of hatred and the apocalypse of Nothingness.

The language of love—of passion fastened to its primary object, God, and thereby controlled and ordered—is sober and free. It deals with every thing on terms appropriate to its rank and status. Yet, while it treats physical problems in the matter-of-fact manner indicated by their nature, it retains the freedom of rising to exalted questions of spiritual life. But this rise does not mean sacrifice of precision in favor of a cloudy pathos. The demand for precision becomes rather more exacting with the greater dignity of the object, though it can no longer be satisfied by simple conformity to teachable rules. And since the mind is at ease in this rising and descending move (compared with its hardest labor, the intellectual quest has in it an element of play), it speaks simply and unaffectedly, and nothing is more abhorrent to it than the pomp of arrogated impersonality or the flaunting of the vain and capricious ego. In one word, the speech of love is an eminently objective expression.

For the Existentialist with his concept of passion as an "unattached devotion" (T. S. Eliot), the problem of speech creates a well-nigh insuperable practical difficulty. Passion with its absolute intensity has at its disposal words of only relative and finite meaning. Since, then, no words

will express passion adequately, the most blatantly inadequate language will be the most suitable vehicle, for it
will make it clear to everyone that the words should not
be taken at their face-value. With their clumsy and pedes-
trian bearing, they confess their own ineptitude and hint
at the infinite difference between ineffable passion and the
linguistic sign. Language, we are made to feel, is a dis-
guise, an artful and indispensable affectation. There is no
better mask for passion, Kierkegaard remarks, than the
style of the business office and the chancellery (*Stages on
Life's Road*, "Guilty? Not Guilty?", Jan. 17). His heirs,
our contemporary Existentialists, follow this precept with
unconscious faithfulness. The modern master of the
"masked style" is Franz Kafka. With the dry and detached accuracy of a legal document, he describes the
things and events of this world. But in their cold distinct-
ness they inflict themselves on our minds with the power
of an obsession. Their senseless obtrusiveness recalls the
pattern of a wallpaper seen during a delirium, or the
mocking gimcracks on the mantelpiece in the doctor's
reception room, fascinating one who waits for a decision
involving life and death, or finally—and this is the fittest
simile—the banal decorations on a curtain veiling a terrible mystery.

The Existentialist philosophers follow suit. Heidegger,
in *Sein und Zeit*, writes with the fanciful ponderosity of a
clerk who has fed all his life on the dust of enormous
ledgers. Yet so fierce is his application that occasionally
he might be taken for an expressionist picture of the
Recording Angel. Sartre in his philosophical writings is
less given to monumental bizarrerie but he is no less
technical, studiedly impassive, and coldly analytic than
his German confrère. But both Heidegger and Sartre see

to it that the heavy apparatus of philosophical terminology vibrates with the overtones of passionate excitement. Death, care, anguish, flight, shame, pride, want, Nothingness—menacing and disturbing words like these set the tone which is that of errant passion.

The third partner in the alliance of contemplation and love is rational faith. In affirming this idea we are at the opposite pole to Existentialism. As a matter of fact, the Existentialist position might be described as the emphatic denial of precisely this idea.

In developing his concept of the concrete individual, the Existentialist faces the problem of reason's impotence as a guide of action. As agents, we must decide here and now, under the pressure and limitations of a concrete situation. Reason, however, in grand detachment from the pressing needs of the moment, discovers (or believes it discovers) the great principles of action within the framework of total reality—a useless discovery as far as the individual is concerned. Acceptance of the idea of ascent mitigates that difficulty but does not remove it. Ascent is a process and, from the point of view of the agent, a never completed process. But the moment for action is now, and the principles to guide it must be available now. At this juncture the idea of rational faith points a way out of the dilemma.

From the point of view of a fully developed Christian faith, rational faith may be called an undeveloped or implicit faith. But it has an explicitness of its own. It is not faith in Christ as God's Son and our Redeemer, but it is faith in a cosmos or creation which as a total order includes the moral order exhibited in our lives even while we violate it; it is faith also in the uncreated Master Mind as revealed in the created order. It is faith in Being, and as such it is diametrically opposed to the faith in nothing springing from the encounter with Nothingness. It is the basis of every theory of Being (ontology) as contrasted with a theory of non-Being (mē-ontology). Yet it is faith, not knowledge. The nature of this faith consists in the leaping forward to a position still beyond reach for the intellect, not, however, considered as a mere hypothesis but held with perfect trust. The incompleteness and anticipatory character of the intellectual grasp combines with total commitment. The acceptance of the idea of rational faith does not entail a philosophy of intellectual laziness (*philosophia pigrorum*)—rather the contrary. For this faith, although more than an hypothesis, has yet the virtue of an hypothesis. It works, as it were, backwards, as a guide to the intellect which lags behind. It does not shy away from reason—rather it clamors for rational verification. It makes relentless demands. These demands are insistent, present now, at every moment, not available only in the concrete situation but constituting it. And among these demands there is also the one which imposes upon us the duty of discovering reasons for what we believe is true.

Sartre thinks it is sufficient for the human agent to cling with determination to the practical rules which he has invented for himself in the same way in which an author in sovereign freedom invents a character for his novel. But this way lies madness. Nothing short of the bedrock of reality will sustain us in life.

The ancient cathedrals of Europe have been laid in dust by modern explosives, and only the excess of human suffering prevents us from indulging in despair over this loss. Also, we reflect that the material destruction is symptomatic of a spiritual disorder. It has been preceded

by the demolition of the principles which, comparable
to pillars, sustain the intellectual structure of civilized
life. The ideas of the cosmos or creation, of the contemplative life, of love as the prime creative force, and of rational
faith, are among the supporting principles. As the Existentialists busy themselves with their analytical tools, we
hear the clicking and grating of spades and that weird
scene of the grave-digging Lemurs in the second part of
Goethe's *Faust* (V) rises before our eyes:

> *Lemur* (solo): Who has furnished the hall so poorly?
>   Tables and chairs—where are they gone?
> *Chorus of Lemurs:* All was borrowed for a short while,
>   And creditors are many. . . .

It would be an injustice towards Existentialism to end
on this macabre note. Grave-digging too is a creative
activity, and to the extent that a theory is destructible,
its destruction is infallibly self-destruction. The Existentialist's message is not devoid of truth, and the particular
element of truth which he conveys is very much in tune
with the stark and obtrusive facts of our time which, as
Jaspers judges, is out of touch with Being (*Die Geistige
Situation* . . . , p. 14). The Augustinian-Franciscan idea of
order remains eternally true (cf. p. 44 above). Yet that
other so-called order of which Aegisthus in Sartre's play
is enamored is much in evidence. The concentration
camp of Dachau was a very orderly place. To the roll
call in the evening even the dead had to be dragged so
that there might be perfect accord between names on the
list and bodies present.

But aside from its timeliness, an ambiguous virtue,
Existentialism has its timeless truth—a truth, perhaps,

which particularly needs to be brought home to man in this historic hour. Frail mixture that he is, "at every second thrilled with being as well as not being" (Paul Claudel, *The Satin Slipper* [Sheed & Ward, 1937], Act III, scene 8, p. 168), he can lay hold on Being only by an option of his soul. The Existentialist prods him and makes it harder for him not to make up his mind.

VI

Condemned to be Free

UP TO THE POINT to which we have followed the Existentialist argument, it reflects a process of emancipation—emancipation from a meaningful and orderly cosmos which could hedge in the individual, emancipation from the tutorship of a constraining moral law based upon the nature of things, emancipation, finally, from God whose authority would exclude every form of freedom except the one that, paradoxically, is called a perfect service.

The individual that accepts and follows through the Existentialist argument must think of himself as free indeed and as in no sense a servant. However, this freedom of his limits itself. He is not free to divest himself of his freedom and not even to suspend it temporarily. He must be free. He is condemned to be free. Nor should the latter expression be regarded as gratuitously dramatizing the situation. The Existentialist finds himself in the open. But whether the relinquished walls should be remembered as a prison or a shelter is still an unanswerable question. The freedom thus acquired is, at first sight, terrible. To be so free means to be determined to Nothing. It is through the encounter with Nothingness that the individual learns about his freedom. Becoming acquainted with freedom is tantamount to despair. Of course, despair is thought of merely as a stage, not as a terminal. The passage through acute despair, we are made to understand, is required that the latent despair might be vanquished. It remains to be seen how that victory can be won—how freedom can become creative.

The emancipation from the cosmos involves the emancipation from objective truth (Chap. IV). With the elimination of objective truth, man is set adrift and no marks for his orientation are left. But again this disorientation, the experience of estrangement, is conceived only as a transition and an inevitable trial. Truth in the objective sense is to be surrendered only to be given a fresh basis in the individual himself. How this restoration of truth as inward or subjective truth is to be achieved, we must now try to find out.

The move which is to have the double result of restoring to freedom its creativity and to truth its validity runs through two phases. The first phase, negative in character, is related to the second, affirmative one as the swing to the throw or the start to the jump. First the bitterness of freedom must be tasted to the dregs, and then, by a sudden reversal, we may feel its sweetness on our tongues. This succession of move and countermove, or of descent and resurgence is a logical advance as from thesis to antithesis, or rather from a tension between thesis and antithesis to synthesis. But the dialectic involved is an existential dialectic rather than a formal dialectic. It reflects an inner drama, and the driving power which brings the drama to a crisis is not reason but passion. Yet the plot of this drama is amenable to intellectual expression. In the present chapter we propose to deal with the first, preparatory phase of the dialectical progress.

The individual who has become initiated into the existential situation through emancipation, finding himself free (and especially free from guidance and protection)—this individual is in despair. The entire first phase of our dialectic is a marking time within the closed sphere of despair. The futility of this restless standstill brings home to the sufferer the necessity, but at the same time the apparent impossibility, of breaking through that enchanted circle. We witness the agony and the spiritual death of the soul, and this death, while its empire lasts, swallows all hope for rebirth.

The despair under consideration, however, is not essentially hopelessness. It is not that most perilous of mortal sins which the Schoolmen regarded as the negative counterpart to hope, one of the three "theological virtues" (cf. St. Thomas, *Summa Theol.*, II-II, q. 20, a. 1). Just as the virtue of hope is confident anticipation of eternal life, so despair as the corresponding sin is the despondent surrender of this hope and acquiescence in perdition. But despair in the mouth of the Existentialist, though it may involve this sin—sin also has its place in the plan of salvation—is basically a different thing. The German word *Verzweiflung* and its Danish equivalent suggest a condition created by the victory of doubt over certitude. After doubt has done its worst, wrenching the mind away from Being and confronting it with Nothingness, then despair reigns. As anguish is the subjective pendant to the Nothingness of freedom, so despair corresponds to estrangement, the Nothingness of the world.

There is no despair without passion, and through despair the dialectical character of passion is revealed and brought into play. In the light of desperate passion the objects of this world and finally the world in its entirety are discovered as meaningless and irrelevant to man. This irrelevancy could not be detected and felt unless passion had its own criterion of relevance. In fact, such a thing as ultimate relevance exists only through passion, that is, through the absolute intensity of desiring and willing. Something becomes relevant by its being related to the object of passion. In despair we discover that nothing either within the world or outside it can assuage passionate desire, and that, consequently, everything is irrelevant. We run up against an invincible incongruity between the nature of man and the world in which he lives. Caught in the relativities of shifting situations, man insists upon the absolute. He is unable to live with this insistence, for the unsolved tension between urge and fulfillment is despair; nor can he extirpate this insistence, because in so doing he would become a robot instead of a man. Accordingly, the dialectic of despair will not be a gradual resolution of contradictions in the progress from thesis through antithesis to synthesis. For such progress is effected through mediation which is here out of the question. Instead, we find an unhappy and inconclusive oscillation between the poles of restless inactivity and listless activity.

"Everything happens and nothing matters." This profession of nihilistic faith renders action futile. There is no sufficient reason for doing one thing rather than something else, nor for doing anything at all. And if something is done all the same, it is done neither for its own sake nor for the sake of the consequences flowing from it, but in order not to do nothing. Action is flight from inaction.

This vacuity of a mind smitten by the encounter with Nothingness is ennui or tedium, in German (which here once more is closer to Danish than either French or English) *Langeweile,* a word which evokes the experience of time as a viscous flow. Devoid of any real filling, time stretches, lingering mockingly as it were before our eyes, yet too quick to be grasped and used, and in stretching, it finally grows into an overpowering reality. Nothing *is,* but everything is continually coming into Being and ceasing to be.

Kierkegaard's idea of tedium or boredom as the human response to Nothingness is anticipated by Pascal's idea of ennui: "The condition of man: fickleness, ennui, disquietude" (*Pensées,* ed. L. Brunschvicg, Paris, 1925, No. 127). There needs to be no particular cause of distress. Such is man's misery that ennui lies at the very bottom of his mind as an awareness of the nought (*néant*) that he is (*ibid.,* 131, 139). This is why games, the company of women, war, and employment in affairs of the state are eagerly coveted. Not as sources of real happiness are they sought, but as *divertissements*—a whiling away of time that otherwise would stretch intolerably, a fabrication of screens to hide the void which yet remains unfilled.

Kierkegaard rings all the changes of the same theme. Boredom, he asserts, is the "root of all evil," and everything depends upon keeping its demonic power in abeyance (*Either/Or,* I, 237–39).

How terrible tedium is—terribly tedious. . . . I lie stretched out, inactive; the only thing I see is emptiness. . . . I do not even suffer pain. The vulture constantly devoured Prometheus' liver; the poison constantly dripped down on Loki; that was at least an interruption though a monotonous one. Even pain has lost its refreshment for me. If I were offered all the glories of the world, or all its pain, I would not turn over on the other side either to obtain them or to escape them. I die the death. Is there anything that could divert me? Aye, if I might behold a constancy that could withstand any trial, an enthusiasm that endured everything, a faith that could remove mountains, a thought that could unite the finite and the infinite! But my soul's poisonous doubt is all-consuming. My soul is like the dead sea, over which no bird can fly; when it has flown midway, then it sinks down to death and destruction (*ibid.*, I, 29–30).

The lordly man as portrayed by Aristotle (*Nic. Ethics*, 1125a) is not easily moved to admiration because he considers few things great. This proud equanimity is caricatured by the great blasé, the hero of boredom, who struts through the pages of Kierkegaard, Byron, Lermontov, and Dostoyevsky, insulting heaven and earth with his insolent and mournful nonchalance. But since we have passed out of the charmed circle of the Romantic emotion, it is not difficult for us to discover the poor taste of these melodramatic impersonations of boredom. We respond more favorably to the less fatuous and more subdued symbols of disgust in contemporary poetry. The bleak defaced cities of the machine age furnish setting and material.

Poets once spoke of love. T. S. Eliot tells us what becomes of love in London, in a cheap furnished room, under the reign of tedium. A "young man carbuncular," "a small house agent's clerk," plays the lover:

> The time is now propitious, as he guesses,
> The meal is ended, she is bored and tired, . . .

Then, after it is over and he happily gone:

> She smoothes her hair with automatic hand,
> And puts a record on the grammophone.
>   —*The Waste Land*, ll. 235–56

Kierkegaard's eloquence in evoking the void is ineffectual compared with this terse sketch of a gesture or with W. H. Auden's drowsy lines on the winter that "completes an age":

> Huge crowds mumble—"Alas,
> Our angers do not increase,
> Love is not what she used to be";
> Portly Caesar yawns—"I know";
> He falls asleep on his throne,
> They shuffle off through the snow:
> Darkness and snow descend.
>   —"For the Time Being," I

The language employed by Existentialists in describing the condition of tedium and the use to which this conception is put by the Christians among them, by Kierkegaard himself, by W. H. Auden, and others, urges upon us the question of whether this spiritual agony is identical with the "mystic death," the Dark Night of the Soul, of which the mystics tell us. The answer is not a simple yes or no. There is a radical difference and this is a fact of primary importance. Yet there is also, at the periphery of the two phenomena, a point of contact and even of fusion, all the more significant because of the antimystic bias of Kierkegaard and the majority of his followers.

The similarity of language is striking indeed. Tedium,

ennui, emptiness—these words from the Existentialist vocabulary are fully applicable to a mystic experience more commonly referred to as the dryness of the soul or acedia ("spiritual indifference") or, with a different emphasis, as the annihilation of the self, or the "noughted soul." The same correspondence of terms exists on the side of the object. God Himself is described by mystic writers as Nought (one remembers the *Gottes-Nichts* in Meister Eckhart), and this divine Nothingness, like the *Nichts* in Heidegger, is active—it "noughts" ("*es nichtet*"), and the fruit of its annihilating activity is, in Walter Hilton's expression, the "noughted soul" (*The Scale of Perfection*, Book II, Chap. 35). The same metaphors are used, especially the dark night, the desert, and the abyss. Tauler speaks of the "Wilderness of the Quiet Desert of the Godhead" (*The Inner Way*, Third Instruction, p. 324); Ruysbroeck, of the "Abyss of Darkness where the loving spirit dies to itself, and wherein begins the manifestation of God and of Eternal Life" (*L'ornement des noces spirituelles*, Lib. III, chap. 2). Tauler and Eckhart play with the similarity of the German word for ground or reason (*Grund*) and the one for abyss (*Abgrund*)—and so does Heidegger (*Vom Wesen des Grundes*, p. 109).

Let it be said at once that the kinship of language is misleading, particularly where the objective side of the experience is concerned. The Nothingness of the Existentialists is the actual void, nothingness by itself, the deprivation of Being or, at any rate, of meaningful Being. But when the mystic speaks of God as Nought, as darkness, or as abyss, he means to say that God appears so to us. The God-Nothing is really our own nothingness which is unable to comprehend God. It is the inadequacy of our own human language which, in the vain attempt to

express God, is finally reduced to stammering "Nothing,"
thus confessing that our words are too narrow to hold
God and that He can be expressed only negatively and
indirectly by the admission of our failure to express Him.
Considered by Himself, God is none of the things he is
likened to. In fact, He is the very opposite, and it is blas-
phemy to think otherwise. God, in truth, is the "rich
nought" that appears void only to our deficient comprehension, the infinite light of wisdom which, precisely
because of its superlative resplendence, is like night to
our feeble eyesight, the teeming abyss of Being rather
than the waste abyss of Nothingness.

The difference or rather the contrast is made superbly
clear in Paul Claudel's *Le soulier de satin* (Act III, scene
10). Don Camillo in this play impersonates undirected
passion which, following its inner logic, must finally
establish the reign of Nothingness, while Dona Prouheze
is the mouthpiece of the God-directed passion of love.

Don Camillo. Is prayer, then, just an avowal of
nothingness?
Dona Prouheze. Not only an avowal, but a state of
nothingness.
Don Camillo. When I just said I am nothing, was I
uttering a prayer?
Dona Prouheze. You were doing the very opposite,
since the only thing that God lacks you wish to keep
to yourself, preferring it to being, and resting con-
tent with your own essential difference.

The anguish suffered by the mystic in the spiritual
desert is still prayer, whereas the Existentialist's encounter
with Nothingness is "the opposite." There is, however,

in the experience of the Dark Night of the Soul another element which is very close to the Existentialist's affliction, the tedium. With his negations the mystic expresses not only the inability of the human intellect to grasp God. Passing through the Dark Night (generally after a period of happy progress in contemplation and nearness to God) the soul is in sore distress. It suffers from a sense of the absence of God, and this primal privation is followed by the loss of all its previous possessions. Its joy is turned into dull helplessness and ennui, its Godward advance into a sense of impotence and disintegration, its sense of shelteredness into desolation. "Even the power of voluntary sacrifice and self-discipline is taken away" (Evelyn Underhill, *Mysticism. A Study in the Nature and Development of Man's Spiritual Consciousness*, [12th ed. London 1930], p. 400). This is truly a state of pain.

The period of spiritual destitution as suffered and explored by the mystic writers bears so close a resemblance to the tedium and fatigue of the soul which grow upon the mind through the encounter with nothingness that it is hard to discover any significant difference. Yet there is one, though it is of such nature as to shade off gradually into indistinctness.

The great principle that the soul must "lose to find and die to live" dominates the Christian mystic's thought in all its phases. It follows that even the dread experience of the Dark Night is seen by him as a stage of the soul's journey towards God. Since it is a passage it can be properly described only in relation to a point beyond itself, outside the domain of ennui. This, then, is the distinctive mark: the view of ennui in Kierkegaard and his followers is taken from the hither side of the spiritual watershed only. It is the condition of dryness, seen from

inside, and merely in its own perspective. It is the dis-
consolate interpretation of the desolation of ennui. The
principle "die to live" is not wholly absent. If it were,
the attempt to communicate the condition of tedium
would be an assault on everyone's happiness. But the
intellectual hold on that unshaken Reality which lies
beyond loss and death is so weakened that deliverance
appears an absurdity, to be hoped for against hope as the
all but impossible thing. Tedium takes on the semblance
of an autonomous condition, independent of a process
which transcends it, the futility in man answering to the
Nothingness which confronts him.

The variety of systems of thought which can be classified as Existentialist requires a qualification of our too
sweeping statement regarding the autonomy of ennui in
Existentialism. These systems range from the idea of the
finality of despair or anguish to a view which assigns to
these negative conditions a merely preparatory role. At
the one end of this scale we locate Sartre with his determined atheism and we associate him with an otherwise
uncongenial partner, Bertrand Russell ("A Free Man's
Worship," in *Mysticism and Logic* [7th ed. London, 1932],
pp. 46–57). Following the advice of these men, we must
try to feel at home in anguish and Nothingness, or at any
rate we must come to terms with them. For it is they that
constitute existence. This was also Heidegger's position
until he became converted to Hölderlin's prophetic promise of the future advent of gods or God. Then follows
Kierkegaard and with him Jaspers, who among modern
Existentialists is closest to the Danish precursor. For both
of them the condition of despair and tedium belongs as
the opening or critical phase in a dialectic which culmin-
ates in certitude.

Finally, in Gabriel Marcel's empirical mysticism, ennui clearly results from an initial error. Once the error is discarded ennui disappears. The error (an error of the whole man and not only of the mind) consists in staying within the sphere of disinterested objectivity. As the tinge of objectivity settles on all things, they become alienated from me, the living concrete man. But I need only to rise to those concrete experiences of participation through which the presence of my fellow man as a "thou" rather than a mere "he" is revealed to me, together with my own presence to myself, and finally to the presence of God, the "Eternal Thou," in order to be delivered from the domain of "Having" and to rejoin the inexhaustible plenitude of Being. To this superabundance I shall respond with a perpetual *encore*, "which is the very opposite of ennui" (*Journal métaphysique* [Paris, 1927], pp. 275–80). The characteristic tension between the "Everlasting No" and a subsequent affirmation is here toned down to a progress in religious-philosophical enlightenment. But Marcel's thought, which has its source in Bergson rather than in Kierkegaard and which was formed under the influence of Bradley, belongs only at the periphery of what is here studied as Existentialism.

To a narrowly technological view of history, the giant cities of the age of industrialism may appear as monuments of progress. To some of the more sensitive among our contemporaries, they are rather the symbolic embodiment of that tedium which first crept into the souls clandestinely and stands now revealed in ghastly obtrusiveness. The Big City, far from being an evidence of successful progress, is seen as testifying to an arrested progress. It symbolizes, not a prayer offered, but one choked off in its inception. In this place of disaffection there is, in T. S. Eliot's words, neither daylight nor "darkness to purify the soul," "neither plenitude nor vacancy," but only a "tumid apathy with no concentration." But even this cruel vision of London is, in the poet's account, introductory to the saving descent into darkness—"into the world of perpetual solitude" ("Burnt Norton," III, *Four Quartets*). Even the desperate hebetude of the soul is not beyond redemption. It, too, may testify to the resurrectional pattern of life, the "die to live."

There is an active tedium just as there is a passive one. The aspect of Naught may paralyze its victim, but it may also hound it in headlong flight around the sphere of human activities. Action, then, is escape from inaction. But it is not, for that reason, feeble or half-hearted. On the contrary, it will be of sinister determination and fanatical violence. Someone speaks and acts with heat and vehemence. Is that a sign of sincerity? It is more probable that he tries to compensate by vehemence for a lack of quiet conviction.

Nothing is worth doing. As passion fixes its glance on the purposes of action such as they offer themselves to the unemployed will, they shrink and wither into insignificance. A modern Cineas, warning King Pyrrhus against the projected campaign against Rome, would have spoken less of the perils of the enterprise. Adopting a prouder language than the sane and soft-spoken Hellenic philosopher, he might have harangued his ambitious master as follows: "A world, my king, is waiting for its master. Stretch out your hand, and Rome will sink in the dust before you, and once she is fallen, Sicily will be yours, Africa will follow into captivity, and the Orient, now rebellious, will offer tribute. But I warn you not to stretch out your hand and to turn a deaf ear on the

clamoring of the world for a lord to subdue it. I know of
the fire in your heart. It consumes whatever you feed it.
Should you deign to listen to the craving of the masses
and throw into the fire of your passion that enormous
log, the rulership over the inhabited earth, only to find
that it too is devoured, and that the fire burns on with
unabated voracity? Spare yourself that disappointment.
Be proud enough to refuse the deceptive glory."

To which Pyrrhus, acting the part of the modern
dictator but with an intellectual lucidity foreign to this
brutish robot of passion, would have retorted: "My dear
Cineas, you try to destroy an illusion which I do not
cherish. That the conquered earth will not be a conquered
paradise, not even the remote similitude of one, I know
full well. I know that the food to assuage my hunger exists
nowhere. But although I know all this, it is my pleasure
to put up with what I find and to tickle my palate with
the little dainties of conquest. So I will not only conquer
the nations living around this middle ocean of ours. I will
build a fleet of triremes stronger than Persian galleys and
faster than a Phoenician craft, and will send it out beyond
the Pillars of Hercules to continents washed by the
outer ocean. And it will not be enough for me merely to
be called lord and master of all mankind, king of kings,
and ruler of rulers. I shall see to it that the men and women, yea, even the children of this era, become truly mine,
stamped with the seal of my mind, thinking my thoughts,
their being reflecting my image, their tongues. . . ."

He broke off, looking with mild surprise and much
satisfaction at his counselor. The learned Cineas had
changed his attitude while his royal master spoke with
growing passion. The assumed superiority of the accredited
teacher and expert in wisdom had vanished, flushed and

trembling he bent his knee, mumbling rapturously: "Pyrrhus, my god, my savior, I have long been waiting for
you" (cf. Plutarch, *Vitae*, "Pyrrhus," *cap.* 14; cf. also S.
de Beauvoir, *Pyrrhus et Cinéas. Les essais.* Paris, Gallimard.)

Our fictitious king has seen clearly why desperate action
—action in flight from inaction—tends to be violent.
There is, to use Kierkegaard's terms, a qualitative difference between that which passion desires and the gratifi-
cations within man's reach—between the absolute and
the relative. The desperate intensity of impassioned action
is a vain attempt to obliterate that difference by quantity.
The prisoner mimics freedom by pacing round and round
in his cell. Moderation is generally conferred upon action
by its goal, for the immoderate pursuit infallibly misses or
destroys its purpose. But passionate action does not have
a real purpose. All its professed purposes are pretexts;
hence the lack of a moderating principle. There is coldness in its heat, for every specific cause or purpose, embraced with fierce intensity, is only a stopgap, something
picked up in haste and thrown away the minute a better
chance for the deployment of energy is offered. Seeing
someone attacking his task with impetuosity, we think,
"He will cool off." Likewise, in observing the fierceness of
a dictatorial government fresh in power, the experts say:
"Let them blow off steam. They will settle down." These
predictions are often correct. But they do not apply to
cases of passionate action. Here the opposite tendency
prevails. Every new morsel of success whets the appetite
for more and more. Far from submitting to inertia, swift-
ness develops into wild precipitation and desire becomes
madness. There awakens that demonic power called by
the Greeks *pleonexia*, the lust for self-aggrandizement, and
described by Plato as the perverted *eros* which with its

sharp sting drives the tyrannical soul into a career of crime and self-destruction (*Republic* 574d).

No goal is really pursued. That which is pursued is the negation of all goals—it is nothing. And this nothing, placed in the focus of the human will, takes on a mock reality. It kindles a cupidity which is the denial and perversion of all natural desires. Nought is coveted as though it were. Love desires the greatness of its object. So also the perverted love: it desires Nothing to be great and to reign supreme; in other words, it desires the destruction of everything that is. A will directed with absolute intensity towards a goal which ought not to be so striven after is called demonic, and at the base of the demonic the fiendish desire for total destruction lurks. It is curious to note that Gabriele d'Annunzio, who in *Il trionfo del morte* celebrates the nostalgia of the abyss, is also the inventor of the ritual of modern totalitarianism.

The demonic man is one for whom the encounter with Nothingness has become a love affair. He is enflamed with the desire for non-Being; or if it seems too absurd to ascribe causality to something which is not, we may, without escaping absurdity entirely, assert instead: he is driven by the fear of Being or of the Good. Kierkegaard has sketched three symbolic impersonations of the demonic: Nero— man in search of sensation; Don Juan—man in search of love; Faust—man in search of knowledge. In all three cases the object of search, measured by the intensity of desire, is inadequate, and so the thing searched for is ultimately the search itself. Furthermore, all three cases are figures of despair: a brooding sense of futility underlies the fierceness of pursuit—the hunter himself is hunted. Finally, all three characters are "tragic" in a perverted sense of the word; they are evil without being mean. Since they are contemptuous of small pleasures, their great suffering is the perverted similitude of the suffering of the saint. They are the heroes and martyrs of Nothingness.

Nero, satiated with the sublime honors of the throne, hankers after the vulgar honors of the circus. He, the guardian of the Eternal City, lusts to become its incendiary. Being a man and familiar with all the sensations which manhood can offer, he is tortured by a desire for the unknown experiences of womanhood and childbirth. Being free, he finds himself a captive of his freedom, and the prison walls which confine him are marked by the dreary round of hunger and satiety—an alternation which can be accelerated but from which there is no escape.

Don Juan and Faust belong in an altogether different rank of the demonic compared with the imperial voluptuary. The media in which they move—the love of man and woman and the pursuit of truth — have a greater proximity to the legitimate object of passion which is God. But this greater elevation which ennobles them makes them all the more fiendish.

In human existence the consummation of bodily life, the perfect union of man and woman, is bound up in various degrees of closeness with spiritual salvation. In the heroic lover this tie is closest, and Don Juan is made of the stuff of which Romeos are made. It is not the body as such which attracts him. The body of the beloved woman is desirable for him only because of the mysterious intermingling of body and soul, of the mortal and the divine. He yearns for the fructifying contact with the soul, the "thou" (to speak Martin Buber's and Gabriel Marcel's language) rather than the "she." But the moment of fulfillment which ought to be creative proves a fall. The rapture of the senses, instead of revealing a new vision, blots out the "thou" of the partner, leaving only the "she," now a total stranger, robbed of the promise which had first clothed her with glory. The promise must be sought elsewhere. The hunted hunter must look for fresh quarry.

"We never search for the things but for the search of things," Pascal writes, thus providing the formula for Faust, the seeker who never finds (*Pensées*, No. 135). Lessing, in a famous passage of his *Eine Duplik* (*Werke*, X, 53), expresses the same idea:

> If God held enclosed in his right hand all truth and in his left solely the ever living desire for truth though with the proviso that I should be in error eternally, and if he then said to me: Choose! I would throw myself with humility upon his left hand, saying: "Father, give! Pure truth, I know, is for thee alone."

Kierkegaard quotes this statement with approval (*Concluding Unscientific Postscript*, p. 97), and a long-predominant interpretation of Goethe's *Faust* took it for granted that the poem was intended to glorify as a road to salvation precisely that endless aspiration towards a knowledge which forever evades us. Yet it is obvious that the search for the search's sake makes nonsense of knowledge, just as sensationalism makes nonsense of enjoyment and as the amorous adventurer destroys the meaning of love.

Knowledge as pursued by Faust, far from breaking through the prison walls of freedom, makes captivity final. The demonic man in the role of the sensationalist or the faithless lover may still fool himself with the belief that through some personal mischance he has yet missed the keenest delight or the perfect queen of love. No such evasion is open to Faust. He knows that he is goaded on

by the longing for a vision which is beyond man's reach,
that man's mind is instinct with nostalgia although it has
no home. It is Faust who establishes Nothingness and gives
away the secret of his fellows in the community of demoniacal obsession. In his mouth language itself suffers perversion. Instead of expressing "that which is," its natural
function, it is so twisted as to express that which is not: it
becomes ironical. For irony is the attitude suited to negative intellectual freedom. Since there is no reliable truth,
no position adopted in earnest, all positions can be adopted
temporarily and playfully as possible points of view. But
when a partner seizes upon the position held, either in
agreement or attack, the ironical mind slips out of it, thus
proving its wretched superiority. The man who is cursed
with this freedom languishes in the desert of sheer possibilities. His fate is that of the demonic man in general:
reality recedes from him.

The Existentialist's inwardness is a room without exit,
and passion, far from forcing the locked door open, only
serves to bring home to the prisoner his desperate plight.
Through passion despair becomes articulate.

Despair, however, is suffering. Should perhaps this
simple remark furnish the clue to the riddle? One test of
reality, we may believe, holds out under existential criticism: the willingness to suffer shows that the sufferer has
his feet planted on firm ground—so someone might affirm.
But on second thought this appears empty rhetoric. The
sufferer may crave suffering and take a perverse delight in
it. The road which is arduous need not lead to heaven. It
may be chosen by one for whom pleasures have grown
stale and who seeks the sharper stimulant of pain. Suffering as such opens no way towards creativity and truth.
No exit is visible anywhere.

VII

The Crisis of the Drama

THE STRUGGLE through the slough of despondency is conceived as the first phase of a dialectical advance. The nadir is reached, and now the upward move is to start. Despair has done its worst, and we are looking towards a happy issue from our philosophical troubles. Spiritual death is to reveal itself as a crisis followed by rebirth.

The dramatic pattern is not equally marked in the various forms of existential thought. It is central in the "crisis theories" as typified by Kierkegaard and, in our time, by Karl Jaspers and the Prostestant dialectical theology of Karl Barth and Emil Brunner. It holds a much less significant place in Martin Heidegger and Jean-Paul Sartre, the representatives of the "phenomenological theories" (a name to be explained in the next chapter). It is even more peripheral in a third type of thought, the "philosophy of the concrete," as represented by Gabriel Marcel and Martin Buber. This last type, Existentialist only in a modified sense of the word, must here be left out of consideration almost completely. As we now turn to the moment of peripety—the "change of fortune" in the Existentialist drama—the crisis theories will move into the focus of attention.

The first move is a preparation for the second move only in a paradoxical way. Its meaning is to block any further advance and so to drive the mind into a corner. When all hope is extinguished and despair sharpened into a fine point, then the great reversal is to come. But, of course, it will not come along the path of normal expectations. The crisis would not be a real crisis and the new beginning would not really be new if the move of ascent were continuous with the previous descent. There must be a hiatus, total discontinuity, a bursting forth into a hitherto unapproachable reality. Consequently, this event is either not amenable to a rational account or it can be accounted for only in negative terms. At best, reason may lead us to the limit beyond which the event takes place. At this critical moment nothing less than everything is at stake for the individual. He has to win a foothold for his existence, or he will be eternally lost. It is a matter for him of regaining inwardly the truth that has been lost in the estrangement from the outer world, and thus to make freedom creative. The question of an authentic or unauthentic existence (that is to say, of a truthful existence or a lying one) is at issue.

The decisive act through which everything is won or lost is called choice—a conception formulated by Kierkegaard and faithfully upheld by the majority of Existentialists. Choice, as the term is generally understood, is the act of giving preference to one among several possibilities or of deciding in favor of one or two alternatives. And since every choice has, at least potentially, a moral significance, the primary alternative, which underlies all other alternatives, will be that of good and evil. Choice, according to this common-sense view, lies between good and evil.

Kierkegaard and his modern followers entertain an

altogether different idea of choice. In the first place, the
act under consideration, they insist, is not to be confused
with those insignificant decisions with which in every
minute of our waking existence we carry on our lives.
Each one of these "little choices" will reveal itself under
analysis as the choice of a means towards a predetermined
end. They give effect to a prior determination which
underlies and guides them. Not with that merely executive
activity are we chiefly concerned as moralists and philosophers. We must rather focus on those cardinal acts on
which our whole existence hinges—the moments which
place us at the parting of roads, and as we then choose,
our choice, the dread Either/Or, will either save or ruin
us. It is this Great Choice which, as the organizing principle, animates the little choices of our daily lives.

The difference between the primary choice on the one
hand and the secondary or executive choices on the other
is, of course, no discovery for which we have to thank the
Existentialists. But they may take credit for recalling and
insisting on this commonplace of moral philosophy at a
time when a complacent philosophy has succeeded in
blurring the fundamental distinction. The distinctive nature of the primary choice is generally brought home to
us by the Extreme Situation whose relevance Positivist
philosophers tend to belittle. J. S. Mill, for example, holds
that situations calling for heroism or martyrdom are
gradually being eliminated by progress and public education. Similarly the citizens of plague-stricken Oran in
Albert Camus' novel *La peste* refuse to believe in the plague
because they have ceased to believe in that extremity of
affliction which we call a scourge. Opposing this complacency, the Existentialist philosopher thinks about an extreme situation, as one who lives through it. Pushed to the

limit of his endurance, he holds, man reveals his nature. Kierkegaard saw the historic hour marked by the final breakdown of institutionalized Christianity and his own life suspended between the alternative of reckless enjoyment, with despair in his heart, and a total devotion to God. This was his extreme situation. Projecting his dilemma into the Bible, he read the story of Abraham and Isaac as though it spelled the question: attempted murder or religious heroism? The German Existentialists of the twenties rediscovered Kierkegaard after war, defeat, revolution and misery had opened their eyes to their own extreme situation—the approaching doom of civilization as predicted in 1918 by Oswald Spengler's *Decline of the West*. Karl Barth's *Römerbrief*, published in the same year, testified to another extremity of pathos, that of sin and repentance. At the same time, Rainer Maria Rilke, the greatest German poet of the era, preached the contemplation of death. God and death, he thought, like two hidden cliffs, were about to break the unruffled surface of our sheltered lives (*Briefe aus den Jahren 1914-1921* [Leipzig, 1937], Nr. 38, 8 Nov. 1915, pp. 85–92). Heidegger finally, his mind vibrant with the atmospheric tensions of the years following Versailles, found his passion for the "one thing necessary" kindled by living through the situation of a factual revolution (*Umsturz*). Whether construction or destruction would result from his absolute pursuit he decided to ignore (letter of 1920, quoted by Karl Löwith, "Les implications politiques de la philosophie de l'existence chez Heidegger," *Les Temps Modernes*, II [14 Nov. 1946], 345–46).

It took another war and the disaster of defeat and occupation to rouse the French to Existentialist wakefulness. We could no longer find it natural to be men, Sartre writes, "when our best friends, if they were taken, could choose only between abjection and heroism, that is, between the two extremes of the human situation between which there is no longer anything. If they were cowards or traitors, all men were above them; if heroic, all men were below them." This is why we have undertaken, he continues, "to create a literature of extreme situations" ("Literature in Our Time," *Partisan Review*, June 1948, p. 638). "My brothers, the moment is come. It is necessary to believe all or to deny all. And who among you would dare to deny all? . . . God today has granted to his creatures the favor of placing them in so great an affliction that they must rediscover and espouse the greatest of virtues which is that of the All or Nothing"—so Father Paneloux, a character in *La peste* by Camus, in his second sermon preached during the plague.

Aside from the centrality assigned to Primary Choice by the Existentialists, they differ in still another and more important respect from the traditional interpretation of choice. It is out of the question for them to picture the fundamental choice in the naïve manner of Prodicus' well-known fable where Hercules lingers between the enticements of Hussy Pleasure and the stern demands of Dame Virtue. In the Existentialist view, choice at its gravest cannot possibly be a choice between good and evil. For there are no such entities or principles existing independently of man and prior to his choice. He is, we remember, thrown into an alien world. No signs, no landmarks are engraved in Being to guide him. He is free in the face of Nothingness. Nothing determines him to move this or that way, to choose one course of action rather than another, and precisely therein his freedom consists. What, then, is chosen, and how can this choice be made? As the idea of choice as choosing between alternatives is eliminated, these two questions are really one and the same.

The answer to the question, based chiefly on Kierkegaard, *Either/Or* (Vol. II,) and on Sartre, *L'être et le néant* (pp. 66–82), is threefold. The chooser chooses despair, or he chooses freedom as the supreme good and, at the same time, the basis of both good and evil, or he chooses himself. These are three ways of expressing an indivisible act. Only the emphasis is different in each of the three cases.

Choice is choosing despair. The formula is misleading, because it suggests that in making this choice we prefer despair to some other possible condition. But this is only a superficial aspect of the situation. To understand it fully we must avoid thinking of choice in terms of an object chosen. In so conceiving it, we inadvertently deny freedom by regarding the chooser as dependent upon something other than himself, be it an external object or an objective frame of mind. In choosing, Kierkegaard asserts, "it is not so much a question of choosing the right." For the difference between right and wrong is discarded by estrangement. It is rather a question "of the energy, the earnestness, the pathos with which one chooses" (*Either/Or*, tr. Walter Lowrie [Princeton, 1944], II, 141). The choice must be made in truth. But since the objective standards of truth are obliterated, truth must be thought of as subjective, as a freely adopted attitude. The only remaining standard, then, is that of intensity. Admitted that man's status in an estranged world is despair, the recovery of truth will come about through the utmost intensification of despair. Despair must be willed or chosen in order to become absolute despair.

Achieving a maximum of intensity, in this case, amounts to a change in quality. Absolute despair, that is, despair freely accepted and willed, is despair triumphing over itself, growing creative, and thereby ceasing to be despair.

We recall an illustration used before and imagine a shipwrecked man adrift in a lifeboat. This unfortunate may despair of being rescued. But while he so despairs, he firmly believes in the value of the life which he is about to lose. This belief, while increasing his misery, prevents his despair from becoming absolute. The negation of the hope of survival is based upon a solid affirmation.

Suppose the sufferer be a believer in God and, at the same time, one whose past is soiled by a hideous crime which he himself considers unpardonable and irredeemable. His despair over his physical plight will then be overshadowed by spiritual despair. Neither on earth nor in heaven is there salvation for him, he holds. It is hard to imagine a despair more terrible than his. Yet it is not absolute despair. Once more his negation is based on affirmation. He believes in a righteous God.

Another turn of the screw: we give our character a child for a companion and condemn him to witness the agony of the innocent creature. Under this new trial he may come to cancel his former affirmations, deciding that life is not worth living and that God does not exist. "To my death I will refuse to love this creation in which children are tortured," he may defiantly say in the words of Doctor Rieux in Camus' *La peste*. Then only does his despair ripen into absolute despair; then only does he reach the point to which Carlyle leads the hero of his *Sartor Resartus* (an Existentialist book, if ever there was one) at the end of the chapter "The Everlasting No": "Though the world be thine [the devil's] I am free and for ever hate thee." Despair is willed, Nothingness accepted, freedom won. What was it that caused all the pangs and the heartache? Nothing. The destruction of objective truth by Existentialist analysis is designed to do for us what the agony of the child does for the shipwrecked man. It is to arm us for actual life as revealed by an extreme situation. It forces us into Nothingness, and by sharpening despair to its finest point breaks it.

By virtue of absolute despair man becomes an existing individual in the emphatic sense of the word. He attains to authenticity (*Eigentlichkeit*) which is the existential mode of truth, the individual's being-in-truth. And this subjective truthfulness is the foundation of objective truth— supposedly objective, we should say; for it is in fact derived from subjective truth and lacks a basis of its own.

Viewed in the light of authenticity, life under the dispensation of incipient despair (and that means, the whole of human life this side of the healing crisis) is sham existence (*Uneigentlichkeit, mauvaise foi*). The individual is on the flight from despair, taking shelter behind empty pleasures, aimless activities, hollow traditions and reassuring myths. But the masquerade is of no avail. Despair, tracking down its quarry, will force him to turn round and to stand at bay. The kinship to Stoicism is unmistakable, especially in Simone de Beauvoir, the moralist of the French Existentialist movement, and it is evident precisely where she attempts to minimize the affinity ("Pour une morale de l'ambiguité," *Les Temps Modernes;* II [14 Nov. 1946], pp. 193–211, esp. p. 197). Like the Stoic, the Existentialist invites us to face reality (which means here: to face Nothingness) and to parry in advance the blows-to-come by a fundamental renunciation—the baptism in Nothingness which marks the Existentialist "conversion." Again as in Stoicism and, we may add, as in Nietzsche, the virtue chiefly needed to do the deed, to accept despair and to pass through the hour of the Great Disgust (Nietzsche,

Thus Spake Zarathustra, Chap. 57) is courage. An appeal is made to the Titanic or self-saving element in human nature. Hence the "broken Titanism" in Kierkegaard and his Christian followers, especially in Karl Barth with his abysmal hatred of nature and natural man; hence also the "straight Titanism" in Heidegger who invokes the spirit of Prometheus and finds existential resoluteness embodied in Hitler's brown storm troops (Karl Löwith, *op. cit.,*p.352), or in Jean-Paul Sartre, Simone de Beauvoir, and Albert Camus, who claim the *ethos* of the fighters of the French revolution as well as that of Kant, Fichte, and Hegel for their heritage, while repudiating the hopes entertained by these, their spiritual ancestors. Sisyphus, suffering eternal punishment for his attempt to emulate the gods, becomes the fitting symbol of desperate fortitude. He knows that the rock pushed uphill with an agonizing effort will roll down again once the top of the hill is reached. But undaunted he accepts the perpetuation of his laborious failures (Albert Camus, *Le mythe de Sisyphe*).

Choice is choosing freedom as the supreme good and, at the same time, as the basis of both good and evil. Choosing despair does not mean preferring despair to some other condition. Likewise, choosing freedom does not mean preferring it to servitude. For neither despair nor freedom can be escaped by giving preference to something other than despair or freedom. In preferring pleasure to despair, my option actually lies with the muted despair that lurks behind the intoxication of the senses as over against self-avowed despair. Similarly, in submitting to servitude I am still testifying to my freedom. I am not free not to be free. I am free only to accept my freedom in the light of my knowledge about it, or else to repudiate it in ignorance of its inescapability. In short, the "choice of freedom" denotes no preferential choice but describes the movement of existence towards a climax of intensity.

To be free in knowledge about one's freedom means to be confronted with the nothingness of sheer possibilities. For if everything is possible, nothing is determined. Somewhat poetically the Existentialists speak of an abyss of freedom and they describe the attitude of one placed at the brink of this abyss as anguish. Freedom is not a condition of man in the same sense in which health, fatigue, or old age are human conditions. Man is not only free—he is his freedom. If, then, anguish is the awareness of freedom, it is equally correct to assert with Sartre that man is anguish (*L'être et le néant*, p. 81). Anguish as the Existentialists understand it differs from fear in the same way in which absolute despair differs from relative despair. In fear we shrink from anticipated evil, and so there is always an object of fear, a definable danger such as being hit by a car in crossing the street, social disgrace as the consequence of violating a rule of good behavior, or eternal damnation as the wages of sin. But as we look for an object of anguish, we find—Nothing.

Fear, aside from being fear of something, is also fear for or about something. I fear for my safety and health, for my reputation, or for my happiness, and in each of these cases the danger is exactly commensurate to that which is threatened or, as we may call it, to the secondary real or imaginary object of fear. If, then, the object of anguish is the negation of all objects, Nothingness, its secondary object, to be of the same order, must be Being. So anguish is experienced in the face of Nothingness about Being, and out of this situation a dynamic character accrues to what is logically a mere negation: Nothingness is experienced as "noughting" or "nihilating."

Jacques Maritain holds that "anguish is worth nothing as a philosophical category" ("From Existential Existentialism to Academic Existentialism," *Sewanee Review*, LVI [Spring 1948], p. 226). But how, then, explain the fact that anguish, inducing a "fury of existence," became through Heidegger an effective tool in "the critical and rational destruction of the philosophical and theological tradition"—this philosopher's avowed purpose? (Löwith, *op. cit.*, p. 346.)

The Existentialists consider anguish the fundamental mode of human existence and, at the same time, an emotional climax. Actually anguish admits of further intensification and then becomes dread or terror. Terror too is of universal significance. It is a total self-loss, though only a momentary one, under the impact of an incomprehensible power: the "nihilating" action of Nothingness assumes the form of violence. Leonard Woolf in a little book entitled *Quack, Quack!* (New York, 1935) published snapshots of Hitler and Mussolini together with an effigy of the Hawaiian war god Kukailimoku, thus calling attention to the striking resemblance that obtains between the facial expression of these two dictators and that of the idol. Both show terror in its passive as well as in its active form. They are terrified and also terrifying. They are masks of Nothingness, and as such they are, in a precise sense of the word, primitive. They show unredeemed humanity naked, in one case not yet clothed with divinity, in the other case ripping off that garment in a fury of self-destruction.

It is quite true that horror, the culmination of anguish, underlies all existence as a continual threat. This is the same horror, called *phobos* by the Greeks, which Plato labored to banish, which Aristotle tried to civilize by admitting it into society as tragic poetry, and which,

gradually receding through the books of the Old Testament
(with the story of Abraham and Isaac as a turning point),
was finally vanquished in Christ. The intellectual expression of this horror is the abysmal pessimism of Silenus,
the earth-bound demon who, captured and forced to
utterance by the foolishly curious Midas, reveals his un-
bearable truth: "Not to be born is of all things the best,
and to die is better than to live" (Aristotle, fr. 44, *Frag-
menta*, ed. V. Rose [Leipzig, 1886], p. 48). To civilize man
means to teach him how not to yield to the temptation of
this horror and to raise the center of struggle and decision
to a level where the horror of Nothingness becomes transformed within the orbit of an affirmative resolve. After
this transformation, horror, the absolute negation, appears
as the lure of evil (and no evil can be discovered except
in the light of the good). The Existentialist, busying himself with undoing the work of civilization which, not without some justification, he deems a failure, reverses the
direction of intellectual endeavor. Like the psychoanalyst,
he burrows into the subconscious and stirs up primeval
dread. With the fervor of a prophet he insists upon the
unum necessarium—the one thing needed—but this one
needful thing is Nothing. Aflame with passion—a passion
for passion rather than passion for an object—he preaches
conversion through perversion. The grain longs to be
crushed between the millstones. "Woe to him who will
not be ground," Heidegger writes in 1923 in a letter to a
disciple, quoting a word of van Gogh's which has haunted
him for years (Löwith, *op. cit.*, p. 345).

Anguish as conceived by the Existentialists is neither
unreal nor devoid of philosophical significance. But it is so
utterly opposed to contemplation, the theoretical attitude,
that the attempt to express it in analytic terms inevitably

falsifies it. For this reason the Existentialist expositions of the Great Choice, from Kierkegaard's *Either/Or* down to the pages on liberty in Sartre's *L'être et le néant*, are as unconvincing as they are subtly stirring. They succeed in building up the intellectual myth of the perverted consciousness. This myth bears no strict resemblance to a particular set of actual experiences, nor is it devoid of objective reference. With subtle persuasiveness it appeals to a dormant power which, if fully actualized, would destroy all intellectual utterance.

The anguished awareness of freedom is also described as giddiness, a term invited by the metaphor of the abyss and particularly rich in suggestiveness. In giddiness we shrink from the depth into which we might hurl ourselves if we decided to do so. But this possibility, representative of my undetermined future, exerts at the same time a fascination over the mind. Repulsion, poised against attraction, results in a condition of anxious suspense—a state of neutrality beyond good and evil. But what then? How can the suspense be released into free movement?

At this juncture, the Existentialist imagery, so far clear and forceful, descends into confusion. The climax is impressive: man is placed at the brink of the abyss of his freedom, oppressed by anguish, and giddiness, the enticement of the depth, plucks at his heartstrings. The dénouement, however, is less convincing. Only one fact stands out clearly: whatever may follow, the sequence stands to the series of preceding steps in the negative relation of discontinuity. The movement of transition is a "leap," not a development. It is impossible to trace its progress or to define its goal, and this its rational unaccountability is its very essence. For that reason any particular cause embraced, any objective pursued, any principle adopted in consequence of that transitional move remains unrelated to the move itself. It is something on which the chooser "hits," a ground upon which he lands after his leap in the dark. So Karl Barth, like Kierkegaard, finds himself caught up by the Word of God; Heidegger, after first acknowledging Hitler as the embodiment of authentic existence, later transfers his blundering faith to the coming gods or the God as prophesied by Hölderlin; Jaspers wins a precarious foothold in the passive resistance of the conscientious objector, and Sartre finally embraces the cause of active resistance to Nazi oppression, and subsequently, after the liberation, the cause of the latest, socialist phase of the French revolution.

In the face of these facts, it is difficult to maintain that Heidegger's adherence to Nazism in 1933 was a logical consequence of his philosophy. Only the illogicality of this step was logical. The mechanism of freedom, anguish, and leap may catapult the individual to almost any position offered by the circumstances. The very language used to describe the actualization of freedom shows the vacillation of thought. Sometimes the move is described as a headlong descent or a "throwing oneself into life" (Simone de Beauvoir), then again as elevation (*Aufschwung*) in Jaspers. On the one hand, it appears as an eminently spontaneous act, expression of self-will and activity at its purest; on the other hand, as the sheer passivity of one who is lifted up rather than raising himself, so that the chooser becomes the one that is chosen. But in any case, through the gaining of a foothold beyond the abyss of original freedom the good, or rather *a* good is posited, and along with it its opposite pole, the evil. Now only does choice in the traditional sense of choosing between good and evil become possible.

Choice is choosing oneself. Whatever the objective seized, the seizure is also self-seizure. Again self-choice must not be interpreted in terms of preferential choice, as though we were free not to choose, or to choose anything but ourselves. Just as we "are" anguish, so, according to Sartre, "we are self-choice" (*L'être et le néant,* p. 393). Even when I suffer, I cannot help "assuming" or choosing my suffering and only thereby does it become mine. "I cannot suffer from an infirmity without choosing myself as 'infirm,' that is to say, without choosing the way in which to 'constitute' my infirmity—as 'intolerable,' 'humiliating,' as 'something to be dissimulated,' as something to 'be revealed to all,' as an 'object of pride,' a 'justification of my failures,' etc" (*loc. cit.*). Compared with self-choice as the inescapable mode of human existence, the saving self-choice which is here under discussion is an intensification to a maximum degree. Through it the self, threatened with disintegration resulting from the multiplicity and instability of its goals, wins a focus. By virtue of willing one thing above all other things it becomes itself one. This unity, far from being externally imposed by an impersonal discipline, is the organizing principle of selfhood, freedom in action, or, as the French put it, *liberté engagée*—liberty under commitment. Christians and freethinkers, nationalists and revolutionists, Germans and French—all the various groups in the Existentialist camp agree on this idea of existential authenticity, as attested by the integration of the self into unity. This very agreement is indicative of the limitations of the concept. It is a formal criterion of human excellence and leaves open the question as to whether there might not be an authentic tyrant or an authentic criminal. Not even the question of human autonomy or dependence can be settled on this basis. Kierkegaard conceives of authentic existence as a condition in which the self "founds itself in transparency upon God," whereas Sartre thinks of it as the action of the fully emancipated, autonomous ego. It is difficult to see how, on Existentialist principles, a decision one way or the other can be reached.

The idea of being one's own self and living one's own life, while limited in applicability by its formal character, is by no means devoid of meaning. The exhortation which it conveys is addressed to an age which labors under a debilitation of will power. Not practical error, that is, willing the wrong thing, seems to be the chief affliction, but the ineffectiveness of will, whatever is willed. With this diagnosis in mind, the Existentialist administers a stimulant which, though it will not effect a cure, may yet be a useful measure of first aid.

Before we continue to develop the Existentialist affirmation, we pause to ask two questions: (1) Is the Existentialist interpretation of choice adequate? (2) Is the Existentialist conversion identical with conversion in the Christian sense of the word?

(1) As on former occasions we find that Existentialism recalls an important and timely truth but that it mars its discovery by its irrationalist bias, that is, by an inadequate conception of reason. Therefore its victories over rationalism are mostly Pyrrhic victories. They invalidate not reason but only an eviscerated conception of reason, formed under the influence of physicalist prejudices.

The rationalist view of choice as derived from Aristotle is expressed by the well-known formula: choice is between means only. The idea is plausible enough. In order to choose between alternatives, I must have a standard by which to determine the preferability of one of the possibilities before me. The standard in turn may be chosen in preference to one or several other standards. But in so pushing back the problem I must come to a halt somewhere. There must be some ultimate standard ("an end") which is not chosen but discovered. This terminal point of reference which makes choice possible may be identified as the Supreme Good.

This Socratic interpretation of choice seems to reduce transgression to a mere error. Knowledge of the Supreme Good, combined with an accurate appraisal of the situation, would ensure right choice. From this extreme rationalist position modern analysts shrink back, and with good reasons. But the position ceases to be absurd if we qualify it by a double proviso.

In the first place, a full and adequate comprehension of the Supreme Good is not within man's reach. We obtain only glimpses of it. In the second place, the intellectual grasp of the Supreme Good is not achieved by the abstract mind as it figures in the positivistic theory of knowledge. Knowledge, in this case and generally speaking, has its existential implications. To see aright is possible only to one who takes the right attitude, and we are dealing with a false abstraction if we think of the vision of the Good as strictly separable from the will directed towards the Good. Right action must not be made dependent upon any speculation which tries to elicit the idea of Good from cosmological, theological, or psychological arguments. On this head Kant, the moralist, teaches a lesson which will not be neglected with impunity. But here again (cf. Chap. V, pp. 80–81) the idea of rational faith proves helpful. Practice actually requires a leap—not, however, a leap in the dark. What is requisite and continually per-

formed by every living man is a leaping forward to a
position beyond available knowledge and demonstrability.
The *point d'appui* so reached by the anticipatory grasp of
faith, intellectually insecure as it is, must yet bear the
whole weight of the believer's existence. His weal and
woe depend on his cleaving to it. But while outstripping
reason this faith does not defy reason. On the contrary, it
insists on obtaining the support of reason. Working backward, as it were, it serves as a guide to knowledge which
follows at its own sedate pace.

Existentialism is right in conceiving of choice in the
emphatic sense—the Great Choice, from which the small
choices follow—as an option of the soul. This fundamental
act is a manifestation of that primal freedom which Jacob
Böhme, Schelling, and, in our own time, Berdyaev, rightly
regard as man's prerogative. Though created for God like
all other creatures, he is not constrained by his nature,
and in that sense he might be said to have no nature
He is granted an option. But making use of that right is
not, as Sartre and his friends believe, a creative self-
assertion but an assertion of the existing Good—an act
of faith. This act is the counterpart and opposite pole to
the encounter with Nothingness. By ascribing meaning to
reality it both initi- ates and guides that quest of meaning
which is philosophy and science. Its intellectual expression
is the Ontological Affirmation, the premise of all metaphysics which posits the ultimate identity of Being and
worth. The premise of Existentialism is the destruction of
metaphysics by means of the Ontological Negation. But
this negation is destructive of all theory and, therefore,
self-destructive. Running counter to Parmenides' warning,
Existentialism begins with non-Being rather than with
Being. It is the philosophy of the mind divided against

itself. In the same breath it denies the possibility of philosophy and affirms the necessity of philosophizing. "The point of view of pure knowledge is contradictory: there is only the point of view of knowledge under commitment (*connaissance engagée*)," Sartre writes (*L'être et le néant*, p. 370). He is right, we believe. But he is mistaken about the nature of the commitment. Committed knowledge is love growing clear-sighted in contemplation, and the contemplative life is the intellectual component of the process through which man is assimilated to God. The anguished vision of Nothingness, however, is productive only of a parasitical knowledge. The "me-ontological system" (the system based on the primacy of Nothingness) is no more than the shadow cast by affirmative ontology, and it owes its existence to the very type of theory which it denies.

(2) Existentialism stands and falls with the idea of a passage from the negative state of anguish before Nothingness to an affirmation. This affirmation must be "critical" rather than "dogmatic." In other words, it must be safe against corrosion by existential analysis. Otherwise we would move in a vicious circle: from despair to affirmation and again back to despair. But the difficulty consists in imagining a position beyond the abyss of Nothingness, in immunity from the virus of nihilistic self-destruction.

Simone de Beauvoir and others refer to this doubtful passage as the Existentialist conversion. An answer to the question as to whether this experience is just another form of the religious and especially Christian conversion is implied in our treatment of the concepts of despair and crisis. So we may confine ourselves to illustrating the two types of conversion. It is clearly a case of difference in likeness.

Beginning with the religious conversion, we imagine a

man waiting for the Last Judgment. Confident and appre-
hensive by turns, he prepares for his appearance before the
Judge. His chances do not seem to him altogether bad
and he begins to collect and organize the points in his
favor into an orderly account. Starting his work in the
morning, the structure is nearly completed at nightfall—
an almost plausible "Apology for My Life." Next morning
he rises with the resolve to put the finishing touch to his
great plea. But with dismay he notices that something is
wrong in the very foundations, and he must start all over
again. So day after day: the night undoes the work of the
day, and there is no progress—quite the contrary. What
first seemed easy to accomplish appears more and more
difficult, and finally impossible. There is no defense, the
guilt is clear. As this insight dawns upon the defendant,
despair overwhelms him. For the first time he sees himself
and he shudders. From this moment on, his attitude under-
goes a radical change. First, all his thoughts were absorbed
by the question of how he might obtain an acquittal, how
God might be brought on his side. Now this ambition has
vanished along with his hope. He knows that he has de-
served condemnation and that he will not escape it. He
has not only sinned once or twice or several times—his
whole life has been an offense to God. A curious reversal
of feeling accompanies this insight. Instead of hankering
after the impossible thing, an acquittal, he now eagerly
and even petulantly desires his punishment. But this somewhat morbid condition does not last. It is followed by a
quieter though still somber mood. Something like hope
seems to have returned. But this is too strong an expression. Actually the new condition, placed as it is beyond
hope and despair, is more aptly described as the total and
confident submission to God's will. Self-will is obliterated

and with the serenity that now fills the mind (not yet joy, but readiness for joy) expectation ceases. The "*dies illa*" no longer threatens with future judgment. God is present and the Now, touched by eternity, is brought to a standstill. The conversion in the literal sense of the word —the turning round of the mind—is completed.

The story of Existentialist conversion begins in the same way. There is again a man in anguished expectation of judgment. While he waits and frets and ponders, searching his past life and weighing his future prospects, a fear creeps into his heart more deadening than the fear of condemnation. This is what he fears: while he sits and waits outside the courtroom, the door might suddenly be flung open and behind the door there might be revealed— not the majestic and terrifying spectacle which would unveil the meaning of the world's history but—Nothing. There might be nothing behind those mysterious doors, and the heart-searching, the scruples, the troubled conscience, the pangs of remorse and the flashes of hope—all this might have been in vain, a misunderstanding, generous and imaginative, to be sure, but also puerile and barbarous. Soon fear and suspicion will harden into conviction and he feels like one awakening from an exciting dream to a drab matter-of-fact reality. He painfully smiles at his past fears and hopes and the quest of a meaning which does not exist. Not even hell holds a threat for him. He has acquired immunity from fear by his encounter with Nothingness. So steeled—— But it is impossible to continue this story. The existential leap destroys the imaginative continuity along with the intellectual one. Every ending and no ending fits, and the reader must be burdened with the task of supplying a conclusion according to his taste.

VIII

Illumination through Anguish

THE FOUNTAINHEAD of the Existentialist teaching on crisis
is in Hegel, especially in the youthful Hegel who under-
went the influence of his friend, Hölderlin. For Hegel the
prototype of crisis is the cleavage of mind (*Zerrissenheit;
déchirement* in modern French writers) suffered by the Jews
previous to the coming of Christ. God was then manifest
to His chosen people as an exacting law. Measured by its
stern demand, natural man appeared in perpetual rebellion against his Maker. There was no mediation between
the Divine "thou shalt" and the human avowal of impotence: "I cannot." In his formative years Hegel experienced and interpreted this unhappy condition in terms
of Kant's philosophy against which he battled even while
succumbing to it. In Kant, too, the moral law was the
antithesis to the unreconciled cupidity of natural man.
So the unhappiness of the dissatisfied Kantian (his own
unhappiness) became fused in Hegel's mind with the
wretchedness of the chosen but unredeemed people. This
was the "existential" problem that lay at the root of
Hegel's philosophical growth.

The solution of the Jewish-Kantian crisis, according to

Hegel's early theological writings, is brought about by Love incarnate in Christ. Through Love, life, torn asunder, is healed and made one. The feud between law and mutinous flesh is reconciled in the divine Mediator. This does not mean, in Hegel's opinion, that the strife of concupiscence warring in man's limbs against spiritual man, is composed once and for all. He rather conceives of the reconciliation through Christ as a paragon or prototype and, at the same, as the initiation of an historical process of universal scope and millennial duration. The paragon, he thought, needs to be embodied in the society of men, its cultural and political life, and many nations in succession have to labor and suffer in order to make the Son of God an historical reality. His own philosophy Hegel regarded as instrumental in this second, progressive incarnation which was history. Through dialectic he endeavored to think the mediation that was lived by Christ. But since thinking is itself a way of living, the dialectical system must claim to be a part of the Incarnation itself, the execution of its meaning in the sphere of speculative thought. Synthesis, the mediating element in Hegel's dialectic, is the logical counterpart to Christ. Man in the role of the philosopher, this seems implied in the Hegelian view, can be saved only by dialectic.

Kierkegaard's thought is largely a protest against Hegel. He emphatically denies the possibility of mediation through synthesis and, therewith, the very principle of Hegel's dialectic. But in rejecting Hegel's idea of the solution of the crisis, he yet retains Hegel's idea of the crisis, and this is a very significant retention. It marks Kierkegaard as an Hegelian, though a rebellious one. His position is dependent on the rationalist-dialectical thesis to which it is an antithesis.

Hegel's idea of crisis centers upon the polarity of disintegration and redintegration. The symptom of crisis is
a painful lack of unity so that restoration (through Christ,
and then through philosophy) will be looked forward to
as a synthesis. This, however, is not the full Christian view
of crisis and salvation. The poles around which the latter
swings are remoteness from God in sin, and nearness to
God in vision and love. This vision and this love, it is true,
engender unity, just as sin is destructive of unity. But by
choosing the integrating power of love for his key concept,
Hegel robs the crisis of its transcendent reference. Christ,
in his early interpretations, is not so much the Son of God
who became man and died to save sinners as the avatar
of the healing powers of life. So the Christology of the
youthful Hegel paves the way for a pantheistic system of
dialectic.

Kierkegaard rejects this Christology as well as this
dialectic. But he does not radically transform the idea of
crisis. He only conceives of it as insoluble. His dialectic
is the Hegelian dialectic arrested after the second move.
For Hegel's rationalist intellectualism he substitutes an irrationalist intellectualism. His philosophically transformed
dialectic leads into an impasse. As a matter of fact, to lead
into a philosophical impasse and, in this manner, to get
rid of philosophy—this is Kierkegaard's intent. If, however, Kierkegaard's analyses are understood as an attempt
to purge the mind of philosophy, we should not ascribe a
philosophical dignity to those concepts which circumscribe
the experience of crisis. In talking about nothingness, freedom, *Angst*, leap, and the like, he uses, we may then assume, a semiphilosophical language to describe an actual
experience. He makes a contribution to psychology rather
than to philosophy.

In point of fact Kierkegaard's arguments move in a disturbing twilight. There is a shifting to and fro from philosophical intent to psychological analysis. But this remark does not apply to modern Existential philosophy. In its chief representatives, Jaspers, Heidegger, and Sartre, the philosophical will is dominant. We therefore misunderstand the ideas of crisis and the overcoming of crisis through choice if we take them as descriptive of certain experiences gone through only by certain individuals but so typically human as to be understood by all. Nor is it the primary purpose of this contemporary crisis theory to outline rules of conduct by enlightening us on the way in which certain inner difficulties are successfully overcome. The fundamental contention is rather that in passing through that crisis an insight into Being is acquired — and this implies an insight into man's place in the world. The winning of a position "beyond" the abyss of Nothingness is to involve a vision impervious to that critical analysis which helps to induce the crisis. This invulnerable vision is rather to emerge out of the crisis, and it must be seized by the saving act of choice. "To will freedom, and to will the unveiling of Being—this is one and the same choice," Simone de Beauvoir affirms ("Pour une morale de l'ambiguité," *Les Temps Modernes*, II [16 Jan. 1947], p. 641).

Like Whitehead, like the Pragmatists and, we may add, like any genuine philosophy, Existentialism tries to undercut the convenient psychological distinction between knowing and willing. Psychology presupposes an idea of man as being dependent for his survival on a certain social and natural environment. The patterns of behavior of this living being can be studied along with the corresponding faculties, and this study may be classified as either psychology or anthropology. But the philosopher is guided by a different interest and he asks a different question. Instead of accepting such an idea of man as is offered to him partly by common experience, partly by the specialized sciences, he subjects this idea to a radical examination. He asks: What is man? What is the meaning of "to be"? And what is experience? The convenient definition of distinct faculties breaks down under the weight of these questions. We are forced into a depth below the differentiation of volition and intellection.

The first volume of Heidegger's *Sein und Zeit* does not include an ethics. But just as little is it to be described as an epistemology, anthropology, or cosmology. The "fundamental ontology" here attempted is logically prior to these classifications. Though it does not expound an ethics, it implies one. Every move of the argument by which a picture of human existence (*Dasein*) in the world gradually emerges is, at the same time, an effort towards authenticity of existence. This is a philosophizing not merely about crisis but out of crisis, an intellectual manifestation of that freedom which is fully actualized only in the agony of absolute despair. Though there is not much explicit reference to crisis in *Sein und Zeit*, it is presupposed throughout. *Sein* (Being) and *Dasein* (human existence) as analyzed in this work are seen in "the clear night of the nothingness of *Angst*" (*Was ist Metaphysik?* [Bonn, 1929], p. 18). The claim is made that only an anguished vision can reveal truth. For Heidegger as well as for Sartre, freedom, far from being expressed in actions alone, is manifest in all acts including the acts of knowledge. Freedom, Heidegger asserts, "is the origin of the *principium rationis*"—the principle according to which nothing is without a "reason" or "ground" (*Vom Wesen des Grundes*, Halle, 1929, p. 38). The world such as it discloses itself to human apprehension proceeds from human freedom, though, of course, it is not created by man.

What is the nature of this peculiar kind of philosophical knowledge which not only stands the acid test of existential analysis but whose light requires to be kindled in the darkness of the crisis of despair? Both the method which guides this knowledge and the impulse which actuates it are furnished by Edmund Husserl's Phenomenology. Heidegger as well as Sartre are Phenomenologists just as much as they are Existentialists. This does not mean that Phenomenology is a root of Existentialism in the same sense as Kierkegaard. Jaspers, for example, owes little or nothing to it. But only through the fusion of Kierkegaard's crisis with phenomenological intuition did Existentialism develop into a philosophically significant school of thought. Thanks to Phenomenology, the *Angst* of crisis becomes philosophically perceptive.

The contribution of Phenomenology will be dealt with under three headings: (1) the "return to the things," (2) the *epoché* or reduction, and (3) the idea of intentionality. Husserl, like Whitehead a mathematician before he became a philosopher, a sober and rigorous mind inflamed by the desire to raise philosophy to the status of an exact science, was utterly antagonistic to Existentialist aspirations. Yet under each of the three headings an affinity of his Phenomenology to Existentialism will reveal itself.

(1) The battle cry of Phenomenology in the first phase of its history (during the twelve years that intervened between the publication of the *Logische Untersuchungen*, 1900–1901, and the *Ideen zu einer reinen Phänomenologie*, 1913) is "back to the things" (*Zurück zu den Sachen!*). The "things"

a return to which is demanded are phenomena—not, however, phenomena in contrast to *noumena* or "things in themselves," but simply things such as they show themselves to unbiased inspection. Accordingly, that from which a retreat is recommended—the target of the critical protest—is the sedimentations of an outworn philosophical tradition, encumbering the mind and blocking the unprejudiced statement of apprehended data. Phenomenology proclaims an act of emancipation. This is its first point of affinity to existential philosophy. Just as Existentialism begins with a destructive analysis of philosophical and especially metaphysical tradition, so Phenomenology, though in a very different mood and with different intent, performs a cleansing operation.

Among the conceptual relics cleared away by the phenomenological purge there are the dichotomies of subject and object, thing-in-itself and phenomenon, individual and general—convenient disjunctions overworked by facile use in the neo-Kantian and Positivist schools. There is no question of eliminating these terms or denying their usefulness. What Phenomenology objects to is their careless employment for purposes of philosophical construction. The method of construction itself, requiring as it does large concepts which may turn out to be philosophical fossils, is subjected to critical scrutiny, and in its place a new open-mindedness is cultivated. We are to see "that which is," combining sensitiveness to every nuance in the field of intellectual vision with restraint in generalization and dialectical construction. "Intuition" (*Anschauung*), a favorite term with phenomenological writers, has no mystic overtones. It simply denotes the attention focused upon that which offers itself to our awareness as immediately present.

A counter example may best illustrate the point. In an attempt to prove the logical respectability of the *Geisteswissenschaften* ("study of cultural life") Heinrich Rickert, head of the Southwestern School of German neo-Kantianism, wrote a book on the *Limitations of the Methods of Natural Science* (*Die Grenzen der naturwissenschaftlichen Begriffsbildung*, 1896–1902). The argument is typically unphenomenological in a threefold sense. In the first place, it begins and ends with a stubbornly pursued dichotomy: generalizing knowledge (natural science) *versus* individualizing knowledge (study of cultural life), thus imposing a simple logical pattern upon a complex situation. Second, a methodological distinction is carried out with little regard for either nature or history as prescientific data. The philosopher is interested in the sciences rather than the things with which the sciences deal. Third, knowledge, instead of being taken for what it offers itself in reflexive experience—a seeing or intuiting of that which is present to the mind—is subjected to an idealist interpretation. Knowing becomes thus assimilated to making or constructing. Thought, out of touch with experience and reality, suffocates in the thin air of abstract methodology, and liberation through a phenomenological catharsis appears as an urgent demand. On the other hand, thinkers like Wilhelm Dilthey and Gabriel Marcel are "phenomenological" in their approach, though they owe little or nothing to Husserl's Phenomenology. Not all were equally in need of this liberator.

Paul Claudel's maxim, "just listen and you may hear," expresses well the ethos of phenomenological research. We remember that the destructive existential analysis, prelude to the encounter with Nothingness, involves a constructive element. *Vers le Concret* (1932)—"towards the concrete"—

is the revealing title of a book by Jean Wahl, precursor, interpreter, and critic of French Existentialism. In undermining objective truth, this analysis develops an idea of the concrete individual, living in a concrete situation and knowing himself as a person through his dual relatedness to the world and his fellow men—the "thou" in relation to which he knows himself as "I." The object-directedness and intellectual sensitiveness which Heidegger and Sartre inherited from the founder of Phenomenology enabled them to develop their philosophical anthropology. Sartre, less original than Heidegger, is to a still higher degree a typical Phenomenologist of the Husserl tradition. His descriptive analyses of the nature of sense perception, of the body which the individual not only "has" but "is," and of the individual's relationship to "the other" belong among the finest specimens of phenomenological research.

A curious contradiction is involved in the phenomenological purge. Those encumbrances which it sweeps away are the ossified relics of a metaphysical or analogical conception of reason. Yet Husserl, far from leaning towards irrationalism, is animated by an unbroken confidence in reason's ability to attain to valid knowledge. His Phenomenology, too, expresses a crisis—a crisis, however, not of existence but of reason.

As metaphysicians we will argue that there must be a correspondence or analogy between the reality to be known and the knowledge of it. Chaos is by definition unintelligible. Likewise, a heap of things blown together by the winds of chance is intelligible only within narrow limits. In order to become the object of rational knowledge, revelatory of a meaningful whole, reality must be intrinsically intelligible or rational. This, then, is what we call the metaphysical or analogical concept of reason;

far from being just one faculty among others, reason, on the strength of our argument, must be conceived as that specifically human power whose operation in a unique way corresponds (or is analogically related) to the structural principle of reality.

This metaphysical concept of reason can be (but need not be) based on a theological foundation. It has been actually so based through centuries of Christian metaphysics, and it disintegrated when the foundation crumbled. It was then replaced by an idealistic interpretation. The structural principle of reality (its intrinsic rationality) was no longer thought of as existing independently of man but as deriving its order in one way or another from the constructive operation of the human mind. The idea of correspondence was not discarded altogether but weakened and reduced to concepts such as the harmony of intelligences in Leibniz and Berkeley or, in the Kantian tradition, the hypothesis of a superindividual transcendental subject. It was the latter hypothesis, coarsened frequently by psychological interpretation, which struck Husserl as a hindrance to impartial analysis, especially in logic, and at which the criticism of the *Logische Untersuchungen* was leveled. But here the contradiction occurred. It was very well to disencumber vision by eliminating unexamined and blindly accepted hypotheses. The problem of reason, however—that is, the problem as to whether, how, and in what sense our ideas have a bearing on reality—would stay with us. As long as it remained unanswered, the phenomena intuited by the Phenomenologist were, so to speak, "in the air," unattached to a sustaining reality and insufficiently linked to one another. Husserl was well aware of this difficulty, as we shall presently see.

(2) The solution to the problem of reason as worked out by Husserl became the foundation of Phenomenology in its second phase, opening with the publication of *Ideen*. This brings us to the much-debated phenomenological *epoché*.

The difficulty before us is not simply discarded but utilized and developed into a method of meditation. The disturbing factor once more is the question of reality. How do the phenomenological data intuited by us bear upon the things in so far as they *exist*? Let us, Husserl suggests, deliberately and methodically remove this disturbing problem from our field of vision. Remove does not mean neglect but suspend. We "bracket" the question of existence by witholding judgment regarding it. This act is called *epoché* (ἐποχή) or reduction. With its help the true field of phenomenological research discloses itself. Thanks to it we are free to let our glance wander over a realm of pure meanings (*Bedeutungen, significations*) and there to discover stable structural features or essences. These essences can be studied as they are, both by themselves and in their relation to other essences, untainted, in any case, by the question of existence.

This splitting up of experience into pure significations and essences on the one hand, and existence on the other paves the way for Existentialism. The Existentialist concept of an anguished vision, a cognition won through, and out of, crisis, can be regarded as an inverted interpretation of Husserl's *epoché*.

Through *epoché* Husserl and his followers try to overcome the "natural attitude" which, dominated as it is by practical interest, emphasizes the "existential" rather than the "essential" aspect of experience. But the adoption of *epoche* has in turn an "existential" significance in the narrower sense of the word. It too requires some kind of "conversion"—a turning around of the whole mind. It is an enfeebled copy of the Platonic contemplation which is vision animated by loving assimilation to the object. It involves a putting out of gear of the practical self, a detachment or self-extrication—and this is the point where the Existentialist transformation begins.

The Existentialist repudiates the claims of disinterested contemplation, and to that extent he must reverse the tendency of *epochê*. Instead of lifting us out of existence into the sphere of essences, he would make us wise by pushing us into the burning center of existence, the crisis of despair. Yet in this inverted procedure of existential analysis, there is also detachment, though of a very different kind. For Husserl, detachment is something between a methodical contrivance and an aspiration to contemplative aloofness. For the Existentialist it is a catastrophe known to us under the name of estrangement. The methodological disengagement of *epochê* is supplanted with tragic alienation culminating in the drama of crisis.

In spite of the contrast of direction, the result in the two cases is strikingly similar. Above all, the illumination through the detachment of crisis, like the detachment through *epochê*, throws its light exclusively on phenomena in the sense of meanings or significations. No contact with a real world existing previous to and independent of the individual is claimed. In fact, any such claim would be invalidated in advance by estrangement which obliterates the world as cosmos. At the same time, the vision obtained through crisis and animated by *Angst* is by no means illusory and of merely private significance. But its truth, understood as the revealedness of phenomena, is, in the last analysis, subjective truth. It receives its authentication from the existing individual. While it is continually to be tested with reference to phenomena, its ultimate validity depends upon the authenticity of the existence which it expresses. And this fulcrum offered by existence furnishes also a systematizing or organizing principle. By being viewed as mine, the individual's, the scattered essences of the early Phenomenologists fall into a pattern supplied by the ordering operations of the mind. Such an organizing principle is still woefully lacking in the Phenomenology of the second phase, and Husserl in a third phase of his thinking (especially in the *Méditations Cartésiennes*, 1932), tries in vain to fill this want by having recourse to a transcendental subject. In this respect the Existentialist version of Phenomenology proves superior by its ability to establish a unified whole of interpretation. But must we not suspect that this advantage is dearly paid for by a subjective idealism verging on solipsism?

In order to answer this question we must turn to a consideration of intentionality, the third constituent feature of Phenomenology.

(3) The idea of "intention" and intentionality has its historical home in Scholasticism. Franz Brentano, Husserl's teacher, revived it for modern philosophy. In all its acts, according to Husserl, the mind "intends" something, and intentionality is the fundamental structure of mental life. Perceiving we perceive something, desiring we desire something, angered we are angry at something, our joy is rejoicing over something, and so through the whole gamut of the mind's activities. The cognitive acts are no exception to this general rule. Thinking or knowing we think or know something. Accordingly, we can distinguish throughout the act of knowing (*noësis*) from the thing-as-known (*noëma*). The former can be likened to a

shaft of light, the latter to the illuminated spot in which the shaft terminates.

Regarding the question of idealism or realism, the idea of intentionality is ambiguous. It can be argued that it provides a basis for the realist position by showing that it is of the nature of the mind to be occupied with something other than the mind. But again this passing beyond itself admits of an immanentist interpretation as though the mind, instead of meeting objects, produced them by inner necessity. Husserl, however, maintaining the point of view of *epoché*, can keep this problem in abeyance. He is concerned with meanings and essences, and the question of existence is not allowed to interfere with phenomenological clarification.

We have likened the "intending" act of the mind to a shaft of light, a metaphor which may once more prove useful. We imagine this shaft as having its greatest luminosity at the center and shading off towards the periphery. The illuminated spot on the screen will then show a brightly lit core surrounded by a halo or horizon of dimmer light which at the circumference gradually melts into darkness. The central core of light, in this simile, stands for that which is directly intended, in other words, for the focus of attention; the concentric rings of the evanescent halo for what is "co-intended." In writing, for example, my attention is focused on the idea to be clarified and expressed in words, while a lateral ray of consciousness picks out for me the paper, the pencil, the letters which I try to draw as clearly as I can. But this central field of apprehension is bathed, so to speak, in the dim and yet pervasive light of a wider awareness. While I am concentrating on my writing I am cognizant, by what Sartre calls *connaissance non-thétique*, of my personal identity, of

my past life and the prospects of my future, of this body
which is "mine" in a sense which alone makes all other
ownership possible, of my staying in a village in New
England, and finally of my being a man, a member of
human society and living in the world. In the life of the
mind nothing is external to anything else. All those ho-
rizons of co-intended meanings, and first and foremost
(though last in the succession of discoveries) the ultimate
horizon of "my-being-in-the-world," permeate and shape
the sharply outlined and narrowly circumscribed group
of objects I am attending to now.

It is one of the achievements of Phenomenology to call
attention to the semiconscious and subconscious elements
which go into the making of our cognitive life. One may
find herein a kinship to psychoanalysis. But the aim of
phenomenological research is rather antagonistic to that
of psychoanalytic procedure. While the latter detects
functional dependencies of thought upon subconscious
drives, the Phenomenologist, on the contrary, is interested
in the cognitive significance of acts which are not explicit-
ly cognitive. He finds awareness embedded in feelings,
moods, and attitudes. So the idea of intentionality, the
constructive element of phenomenological method, is wid-
ened and enriched with a new perceptiveness by the
concept of the horizon as the co-intended. Neither Heidegger's nor Sartre's work is imaginable without that
methodological tool forged for them by Husserl. Of course,
his lessons had to be adapted to the new Existentialist
purpose. In the process of adaptation, Heidegger developed out of Husserl's intentionality two new concepts:
projection (*Entwurf*) and transcendence. Both were to become fundamental, first in Heidegger's thought, and then
in that of Sartre.

Project is Husserl's intentionality made dynamic and expansive by transfer from the aloofness of *epoché* to the center of existence which is crisis and anguish.

Suppose I plan to build a house. That is to say, I "intend" the house as something-to-be, and I call this creative anticipation "project." Every step towards actualizing the plan will then be guided and determined by the project. In other words, the one dominant intention will encompass and organize the partial intentions presiding over the various acts through which the plan is being carried out. We may still refer to the dominant intention as the "horizon"—the outer sphere of co-intendedness, but the simile of the cone of light requires qualification to be applicable. For the encompassing intention, the project, while it may recede into the twilight of mere co-intendedness (once construction is under way, we need consult the blueprint only intermittently), is yet the formative principle. The illuminated field is organized from the periphery towards the center. The more determining factors are those which move least frequently into the focus of attention.

Our illustration is taken from the technological sphere. Building is a way of dealing with things under the guidance of a purpose. For Heidegger, and after him for Sartre, this sphere is representative of the way in which the environing world (*Umwelt*) is generally disclosed to man. It reveals itself, as a powerful chapter in *Sein und Zeit* (pp. 66–113) shows, not as a collection of objects but as something to deal with, as the stuff out of which something can be made, as *Zeug*, as a "totality of utensils" (*L'être et le néant*, p. 251). In its analysis of the natural world picture, Existentialism appears as a radical pragmatism.

We miss the point in Heidegger's and Sartre's argument

if we think of "building" in our illustration as a practice
in contradistinction to theory. The activities of making,
using, constructing, and the like; in short, the purposive
dealing with things, must be thought of as animated by
its own awareness. As we have learnt on a former occa-
sion (pp. 46-47) the hammer is perceived as "something
with which to hammer," the land surface of the globe as a
habitable continent, the river as a frontier or an artery
of traffic. The nature of the utensil with its characteristic
teleological structure (the *"um . . . willen,"* that is, "for
the sake of . . ." which determines all doing) extends,
according to Heidegger and Sartre, over the whole of
experience. So the idea of project, developed by means
of a technological illustration, the construction of a building, can be universalized. Instead of saying with Husserl
that I am aware of my explaining and writing down a
philosophical thought "within the horizon of the world,"
I may now, with a shift of language to Heidegger, prefer
to say "within the world as projected by me." Thus the
idea of horizon, just like that of intentionality, becomes
dynamic by being put in touch with that center of power
which is Man in Existence.

Experience as a projected whole is for Heidegger struc-
tured and unified by a purposive intent—the "for the sake
of . . ." or "with a view to. . . ." This structure, like every
teleological arrangement, requires an ultimate, unifying
principle, an end towards which aspiration is directed, or
an ultimate object for the sake of which everything else
is done. In the Platonic tradition the constructive principle
is afforded by the Sovereign Good; in Existentialism by
existing man, or Existence in the emphatic sense of the
word. The formula, "Man as existing projects the world
in which he finds himself" can now be transformed into:

"Man as existing projects himself as a being in the world."
The outgoing movement of projection—the movement
through which world is revealed or through whith it
"worlds" (*weltet*)—returns upon its point of departure, the
self. The existing self is that ultimate end for the sake of
which world is unveiled. Self-projection, involving as it
does projection of a world, is identical with self-choice.
And this self-choice is, as we remember, the choosing of
despair. The vision of the world as self-projection sheds
upon things the somber clarity of disillusionment or
despair. The illumination which it brings on is the
illumination of anguish.

World and existence as revealed to this vision are permeated by Nothingness (*Nichtigkeit*), and the seal of
Nothingness for every living individual, according to
Heidegger, is his own death, certain as fact but uncertain
as to its date and therefore ever present. Only by resolutely
anticipating death—every one his own death—do we acquire the double gain: a truthful vision of the world
projected unto Nothingness, and self-possession in the
authenticity of existence. The gain is not easily won. With
violent determination the individual must emancipate
himself from the superficiality of what people ("*man*")
think and say, the "public prattle" (*öffentliches Gerede*) that
covers up reality. He must train himself to see all by himself his own death and, through death, truth. The undaunted acceptance of his finiteness is to open his eyes.
Heidegger does not have the accents of languor with
which the longing for death is expressed in Novalis or
Rilke. He rather seems to commandeer our thoughts into
a macabre discipline.

The individual, in projecting himself, can arrive at
himself only through an enormous detour. In making this

detour he projects the world. So it is also true to say, according to *Sein und Zeit*, that man arrives at himself only through the world. But just as the world as cosmos or creation is ambivalent—a ladder towards God as well as a temptation which arrests ascent—so also this Heideggerian mock-world. Its temptation consists in the false pretense of objectivity with which it confronts us. It becomes instrumental in self-choice only as we see through its puffed-up nullity (*Nichtigkeit*) to discover and face Nought itself.

So the self presents itself as a movement away from itself—and this movement must be curbed and forced to return upon its point of departure. In this "away from itself" a phenomenological observation and an existential motif are blended. The phenomenological observation is the one that underlies the idea of intentionality and its successor-term, project. The self, as Heidegger puts it (and Sartre follows suit) is "ek-static," and this "tending beyond itself" unfolds itself as time, the fundamental mode under which world exists. The Existentialist world, like creation in metaphysics, is temporality, not, however, as the "moving likeness of eternity" (in Plato's famous phrase, *Timaeus* 37d) but as the externalization (the "worlding") of "ek-static" existence. There is no eternity for Heidegger. As A. N. Whitehead titled his chief work *Process and Reality*, so Heidegger called his *magnum opus: Being and Time*, for which he later, changing the word order, wrote: *Time and Being* (*Platons Lehre von der Wahrheit. Mit einem Brief über den Humanismus!* [Bern, 1947], p. 72). The two titles are almost interchangeable. Both Whitehead and Heidegger express an emphatic denial of static Being in favor of a dynamic reality. But in Whitehead the world process embraces human existence, in Heidegger it *is* human existence. This centrifugal, "ek-static" move of projection, cosmogonic in significance and phenomenological in origin, is then subjected to an existential interpretation. Heidegger speaks of the *Verfallen* of existence—"a falling away from itself and coming under the spell of what it is not"—and Sartre of the "flight" (*la fuite*) of the For-itself (*le pour-soi*) into the By-itself (*l'en-soi*).

A similar welding of phenomenological description with Existentialist interpretation is found in Heidegger's conception of care (*Sorge*). Existence, according to him, is essentially care. On the one hand, this is another expression for the utensil character of the projected world. The perceptive attitude towards this world is a "taking care of" (*besorgen*) something. On the other hand, this outgoing, formative movement is returning upon itself as a "caring for . . ." in the sense of "concern for. . . ." And the ultimate object of concern for existence is existence itself.

Even the term transcendence is forcibly bent by Heidegger so as to fit the circularity of existence. Literally transcendence means a "stepping across" or a "passing beyond." That which is overstepped in the move of transcendence is, according to traditional metaphysics, the sensible world or nature, and the goal of the movement is God. Heidegger makes the same term mean the passing of existence beyond itself to objects other than itself. So it becomes closely linked with the idea of projection, and it must follow the reflexive curve of this its twin concept. That is to say, the goal of the transcending movement is not in the world of objects but in the self. Existence transcending itself traverses the world to return to itself.

Heidegger has repeatedly repudiated the imputation of

atheism, in *Vom Wesen des Grundes* (p. 28, note) and more recently in an interview where he said that, while not denying God, he stated his absence: "My philosophy is a waiting for God" (*Partisan Review*, April 1948, p. 511). We need not quarrel with this assertion. But we must note that it is difficult to imagine a more effective exclusion of God from human vision than is achieved in *Sein und Zeit*. The idea of transcendence, ancient bridge connecting this world with God, is so twisted as to become the basis of finitism. The circuit of power that is to proceed from God to His creatures and back to Him is enclosed within the walls of human finitude. In Kierkegaard's terms, this is a philosophical expression of the demonic, the language of passion locked up in the chamber of inwardness.

Sartre accepts Heidegger's method and conclusions with a number of modifications. The most important of these is the incorporation of a dialectical scheme in the Heideggerian system of "projections"—a trait which confers upon Sartre's work a tinge of Hegelianism. Actually, Sartre is closer to Fichte than to Hegel. As Fichte in the *Wissenschaftslehre* begins with the ego that produces the non-ego and then makes these two terms operate against each other and progressively determine each other in a dialectical seesaw, so Sartre uses being-as-object, or the In-itself, and being-as-subject, or the For-itself, as his antithetical counters. The former he decides to call Being, the latter Nothing, which is rather odd. For nothing can be said about the In-itself except that it is—it is ineffable, devoid of quality and action—whereas a great deal is being said about the For-itself—it is free action and by its "noughting" (*néantisant*) becomes responsible for the whole world. To affirm, as Sartre does, that be-

cause the self knows itself, it (as knowing) is not what it is
(as known) and that it, therefore, is Nothing seems sheer
sophistry. The plain conclusion to be drawn from the
722 pages of *L'être et le néant* is that only Nothing is—a
modern counterpart to Georgias's affirmation: nothing Is.

But let us turn from the imitator to the more serious
original. This is the question which Heidegger leaves
unanswered: how can the "anguished vision" of a projected world such as he develops claim universal validity?
Every discourse carried on with a view to expressing truth
accessible to others and submitted to their free judgment
presupposes an idea of reason. This is true also of Heidegger's exposition. Yet reason is excluded from his scheme
of things. The difficulty is concealed by a dubious strata-
gem. In *Sein und Zeit* Heidegger does not speak of the self
or ego, although the ethos of a philosophy which places
the whole burden of life on the solitary individual would
seem to require him to do so. Instead he sees existence
embodied in *Dasein* ("being-there")—a mode of being
in which all existing individuals are supposed to share in
some unexplained way.

It might be urged against this argument that it is based
on an idealist misinterpretation of Heidegger's thought.
In fact, Heidegger makes it amply clear that projection
is neither representation (*Vorstellung*) nor creation. To
project means for him to unveil that which meets the eye
(*das Begegnende*) or that which, thanks to our projection,
reveals itself. So he tries to maintain a position beyond
the controversy of idealism *versus* realism. He goes even
farther. Not only does man project himself as being in
the world. He in turn, Heidegger teaches, is projected or
thrown (*geworfen*) into the world, and it is now Being that
does this, and ultimately all, projecting. Being (*Sein*), the

counterpart to the Encompassing (*das Umgreifende*) in Jaspers, is strictly distinguished by Heidegger from the Being Things (*Seiendes*). The confusion combated throughout the pages of *Sein und Zeit* consists in misunderstanding *Sein* as a comprehensive *Seiendes*, and the science which the book undertakes to outline is a Fundamental Ontology (*Fundamentalontologie*), that is, a theory of Bieng as such. Throughout Heidegger's later writings this idea of Being increases in importance though not in clarity. Finally it gets the better of the elements borrowed from Kierkegaard, and (human) existence and knowledge appear then as a "clearing" (*Lichtung*) produced in Being. An inspiration derived from the pre-Socratics and coalescing with Hölderlin's pagan eschatology relegates crisis and anguish into the background. Being overshadows existence.

Our concluding chapter will try to throw some light on the eclipse of Existentialism in the thinking of the Existentialists.

IX

Beyond Crisis

IN A GOOD DRAMATIC scene a reversal of situation takes place. The attitude of the main characters towards themselves and each other not only changes, but the final configuration is the antithesis to the one with which the scene opened. The man who steps forth proudly is humbled and confused, the seemingly defeated has recovered his strength, and the enraged avenger is in a soft and forgiving mood.

Existentialist philosophy is dramatic in structure. It too brings about a reversal of situation. It begins with destructive criticism that prepares the crisis, and the crisis, in turn, preludes a movement towards reconstruction. Descent to the nadir of despair is followed by ascent to a new and supposedly unassailable position.

However, the virtue of drama is the vice of philosophy. Philosophy as a theory is debarred from being dramatic. It must be consistent with itself, and it achieves this oneness through the operation of principles sustained from beginning to end. A theory may cause a reversal of attitude in those who become acquainted with it, but it is absurd to think of it as engaged in a reversal. The reversal, in this case, would have to reverse the theory, which means: the theory would cease to be itself.

Applying this to the problem at hand, we find Existentialism confronted with the following dilemma. The theoretical position attained through crisis will either be able to integrate, that is, explain, the crisis or it will not be able to do so. In the first case, the crisis as explained would cease to be a crisis in the Existentialist sense of the word. For this crisis involves total loss of certitude, and the discontinuity of a "leap" disrupting theoretical coherence. In the second case, we would not have one theory but two logically irreconcilable theories: a prior theory which crumbles under existential analysis, and another one which springs from crisis.

Kierkegaard seems to be more keenly aware of this dilemma than some of his modern followers. He escapes it by limiting direct utterance to the enunciation of his final, Christian conviction while he puts his existential analysis into the mouths of fictitious characters. For the same reason novel and drama provide the fittest medium for the expression of Existentialist thought. Franz Kafka's novels, *The Trial* and *The Castle*, contribute more towards an understanding of the Existentialist crisis than the three volumes of Karl Jaspers' *Philosophie* (1932), and Jean-Paul Sartre's play *The Flies* is a perfect illustration of the Existentialist conceptions of freedom and choice. A power remotely suggested in the theoretical writings of the school becomes here a startling presence: Primitive Terror. In Kafka's novels terror takes over the function of conscience; in Sartre's play it is defied. Certain limits, it is true, seem to constrain even imagination in the attempt to give to crisis a local habitation in human characters. The Existentialist novelists and playwrights have so far failed to create the Existentialist Man. K., the hero of *The Trial* and *The Castle*, is a bundle of obstinate and un- repentant anxiety rather than a living character; and Orestes in *The Flies* is even less a being of flesh and blood. Albert Camus who, in *La peste*, tries to draw the figure of the "saint without God," impersonated in Tarrou, suc- ceeds only in depicting a magnanimous crank. Meursault, hero of *The Stranger* by Camus, Roquentin in Sartre's *La nausée*, and Mathieu in his novel, *Age of Reason*, are all flitting shades, suggestions of the nothingness that man is supposed to be and therefore themselves nothing. This defect is partly compensated for by an impression of the spontaneity and complexity of the moving patterns of life which these writers convey, though they are less successful in this than their American models, Dos Passos, Heming- way, Faulkner, and Steinbeck (*cf*. Jean Bruneau, "Exist- entialism and the American Novel," *Yale French Review*, I [July 1948], 66–72). The American novels so highly admired by our Existentialists are written by authors who are not intellectuals, while their own novels are written by intellectuals embarrassed by their intellect.

What we are concerned with here, however, is not thought in imaginative garb but thought in its own me- dium, subject to the law of contradiction. And for logical thought, the dilemma created by the Existentialist "leap" is inescapable. Every attempted escape becomes an escape from Existentialism itself. As a matter of fact these escapes abound. It is one of the characteristics of Existentialism that its adherents are continually on the verge of apostasy. Therefore they offer an elusive target to philosophical criticism. When criticism hits the bull's eye of the Exist- entialist pattern of thought, every individual member of the sect will say that he is unharmed because he is already elsewhere. The apologists are generally right, though perhaps not entirely right. For even while slipping away from the Existentialist source, they continue to draw upon it. Theirs is a case of *mauvaise foi*.

The retreat from Existentialism, no matter whether avowed or unavowed, is chiefly into (1) historio-theology, (2) idealism, (3) Christian theology.

(1) The phenomenological concept of intentionality, we remember, leaves in balance the debate between idealism and realism, and Heidegger's "project" (*Entwurf*) maintains this ambivalence. The self-projection is paradoxically spoken of as an unveiling of that which is. In this bipolar statement of the situation of knowledge the emphasis on the second pole, that of Being, is strong in *Sein und Zeit*, and it gathers momentum through Heidegger's subsequent publications. The philosophical locus of this Being (*Sein*) is defined by a sweeping negation: Being is neither a being thing (*ein Seiendes*) nor must it be thought of as conforming to any one type of being things, be it *Dasein* (being-as-subject) or mundane being (being-as-object). Yet it is the Being of being things, related to them as the determining to the determined, or the constituent to the constituted. But with all this we are still in ignorance of the nature of Being considered in itself.

This much is certain: Being for Heidegger cannot possibly be what it is in Sartre: a "massive plenitude of positivities" (*L'être et le néant*, p. 153), self-contained and attacked, as it were, from outside by the active nothingness which is man. Being, according to St. Thomas, is an act, and in this respect, Heidegger follows the Aristotelian-Thomistic tradition; whereas Sartre, caricaturing rather than following the Hegelian idea of the negative power of the concept (*Begriff*), hands over activity to "active

Nothing" (*néant néantisant*). The dynamic Being in Heidegger will be found in existence, that is, in man, rather than outside him. The unveiling of *Sein* in *Sein und Zeit* proceeds by first studying *Dasein* (the human mode of being). Are we, then, allowed to identify Being as act or activity with that "primal history" (*Urgeschichte*) which is the history of human freedom in action—history, that is to say, as compounded of all those acts of transcendence-decision through which world is "founded"?

The identification of Being with history (the latter having *Urgeschichte* for its living core) is not justified by the texts. It would involve an idealism which Heidegger repudiates. Instead, we may say that, according to Heidegger, Being is revealed in history, and that this historical self-revelation is the history of Being itself. With the adoption of this view the Existentialist search has run full orbit. It returns to the same Hegel in revolt against whom Kierkegaard had once formulated his Existentialist protest. Heidegger, so we learn from one of his students, once expressed the view that the true posterity of Hegel was still to come (*Le choix, le monde, l'existence*, by Jean Wahl, A. de Waelhens, and others [Paris, Cahiers du collège Philosophique], p. 82)—a very revealing remark. The defiant assertion of titanic freedom is followed by a lapse into servitude under a deified history.

But how can this conception of history as the self-revelation of Being be given a concrete meaning that would link it with history such as we actually know it? The role of the purveyor of meaning in Heidegger's development is played by language. Speech, according to *Sein und Zeit*, is the articulation of man's self-awareness in the world: "he is the being that speaks" (*Seiendes, das redet*, p. 165). Through speech, then, there may appear amidst the flux of history that truthful articulation of meaning which confers meaning upon the flux itself.

Was bleibet aber, stiften die Dichter.
That which abideth is founded by poets.

Heidegger accepts the idea expressed in this line by the poet, Hölderlin, and he also accepts the poet's message. Hölderlin's late Pindaric poetry becomes for him a document of revelation. The return to Hegel, carried one step further, takes him to the source of Hegel. For it was through the contact with Hölderlin, in the years of their friendship in Frankfurt, that a vision of history was kindled in Hegel's mind.

Once, in the happy days of Greece, gods mingled with mortals. Then came Christ, "the last of the Olympians," and after him the heavens receded from earth, the temples fell in ruins, the altars stood deserted, and a cold silence fell upon men. In this night the poet raises his voice. For his eye has perceived the dawn of a new day, and the angels of the fatherland, ministering to him, have given him a song on the return of the gods. In his more recent writings, Heidegger embraces this poetical prophecy of Hölderlin. At the same time, he divests himself of the terminology of philosophy and metaphysics which, he holds, perpetuates Plato's departure from ontological truth—his subjection of Being and truth under the "yoke of *idea*" (*Platons Lehre von der Wahrheit*, p. 44). As the "stabilized fundamental structure of Being" (p. 49) of traditional metaphysics, dominant through two millenniums, is now on the decline, Heidegger feels free to return to the semipoetical, authoritative speech of the pre-Socratics. Basing his authority on the authority of the poet, he waits for the absent God to return. But how does he expect to recognize Him? It is not clear from his writings whether he has come to know the marks by which the Divine can be told from the demonic.

(2) Heidegger in his postwar publication rejects for his philosophy the title Existentialism. A new historico-theological faith derived from Hölderlin relegates crisis and kindred notions to the background. But the inevitable lapse from unalloyed Existentialism is noticeable also in those who continue to claim the title.

Heinrich von Kleist as a very young man locked himself up in his room and decided not to let himself out again until he had made up his mind as to the philosophy of life which he should adopt. But the experiment proved a failure. This story may illustrate the point which I wish to make.

It is possible, and even necessary, to resolve this or that according to the situation through which I live. And even if I suspend resolution, suspense is something decided upon by me. But it is highly doubtful whether I can resolve to be resolved, even more doubtful whether it is meaningful to raise the resolution to be resolute to the rank of the First Maxim of living. This, however, is done by Existentialism. Resoluteness may be a desirable condition. Perhaps we should even class it among the virtues. But virtues in general, as moralists agree, can be acquired neither piecemeal nor by directly aiming at one of them. Is not a weakling a person promising himself at every street corner that this time surely he will be adamant? By the same token a philosophy of resoluteness is under suspicion of being an irresolute philosophy.

Jaspers calls the situation of crisis *Grenzsituation* ("limit-situation"), because it brings home to us the insurmountable limitations of our finiteness. The experience of going through the crisis he describes as *Scheitern*, that is, a shipwreck. Sustaining beliefs, he implies, are to be likened to a ship in which we sail the ocean of life. This craft must founder, for the wisdom we need is that of a drowning man. The concluding experience, finally, through which we emerge from the catastrophe of "foundering" is termed an "elevation to transcendence" (*Aufschwung in die Transzendenz*).

The argument against the determination to be determined applies with even greater force against Jaspers's idea of the happy calamity of a shipwreck. For anyone setting out for a voyage it is wise to anticipate the possibility of disaster. Compelled by an urgent purpose he may risk the voyage even when possibility becomes probability. But if disaster is certain, both voyage and shipwreck are no longer possible, or they are so called only in a Pickwickian sense. The enterprise actually becomes an experiment in survival through submersion. The difficulty can be expressed as a dilemma. By definition crisis can overtake only one who believes. But the anticipation of crisis is incompatible with belief. Hence, by embracing a philosophy of crisis I acquire immunity from suffering a crisis. Consequently this philosophy, in a curious reversal of purpose, will tend to create complacency rather than fortitude. The Existentialist resembles the captain who scuttles his ship in foresight of inevitable shipwreck.

It is not clear whether Jaspers is aware of this paradoxical implication of Existentialism. Simone de Beauvoir assuredly is, but she finds no harm in our conclusion. On the contrary, she is happy over it. Comparing Husserl's *epoche* with Existentialist conversion she writes: "Just as the phenomenological reduction avoids the errors of dog-

matism by suspending every affirmation concerning the
mode of reality of the external world while there is no
question of contesting its factual existence, so also does
the existential conversion not suppress my instincts, desires, projects, passions. It prevents only every possibility
of failure (*échec*) by the refusal to posit as absolutes those
ends towards which my transcendence launches itself and
by seeing these ends in connection with the freedom that
projects them" ("Pour une morale de l'ambiguité," *Les
Temps Modernes*, II [14 Nov. 1946], p. 197). A new paradox:
the same philosophy which writes "decision and commitment" on its banner recommends noncommitment as an
insurance against failure. But is this not tantamount to
advocating a Philosophy of Disloyalty?

In order to do justice to Jaspers we must emphasize the
concluding phase of the crisis as conceived by him: the
deliverance from despair by "elevation" (*Aufschwung*).
Through this experience the "Encompassing," unattainable by scientific and discursive knowledge, is apprehended. Transcendence is the name given by Jaspers to
this translogical apprehension. It is again possible to speak
of God, salvation, immortality. But these terms do not
denote objects; they are intimations of the unobjectifiable.
They are signs of a code (*Chiffern*) which must be de-
ciphered by the sufferer of the crisis in the clear night of
despair, and metaphysics is the art of deciphering.

Kant set limits to knowledge in order to make room
for faith. Jaspers resumes this Kantian enterprise, replacing the duality of thing-in-itself and phenomenon with
that of the Encompassing and the objects. But whereas
Kant's concept of faith has a narrow but clearly defined
meaning accruing to it from the ethics of the good will,

transcendence in Jaspers discloses a realm of inwardness (*Gemüt*) which is as wide as it is amorphous.

A return to Kantian idealism is equally clear in the French writers when they are occupied with solidifying a position beyond crisis. Sartre sketches the outlines of an ethics on two different levels, the one speculative and abstract, the other concrete and popular.

First, in *L'être et le néant*, we find a speculative theory of value reminiscent of Fichte and Schelling (in his earlier stage) rather than of Kant.

We remember the fundamental antithesis in Sartre: the Nothingness of the For-itself is opposed to the Being of the In-itself. The former "is" not—it exists. In continual acts of free self-transcendence, it projects the world and itself as being-in-the-world by attacking the density of Being with its negations. And these negations, in turn, spring from the fundamental Nothing which the For-itself (existing man) is. So the active Nothing of existence gives rise to that which is what it is only by *not* being some other thing.

The For-itself (*pour-soi*) suffers the duality of For-itself and In-itself (*en-soi*) and incessantly strives to overcome it in acts of self-transcendence or self-surpassing (*dépassement de soi-même*). "The reality which is man is suffering in its very being. For as it emerges into being it is perpetually haunted by a totality which it is and which, at the same time, it is unable to be, because it could not attain [the status of] the In-itself without forfeiting its status as For-itself. So it is by nature an unhappy consciousness without the possibility of escaping the condition of unhappiness" (*L'être et le néant*, p. 134). This unattainable totality in so far as it haunts "the heart of the For-itself," this want which underlies all our wants, is the value (*ibid.*, p. 137).

One wonders how this concept of value, conceived in the spirit of abstract idealism, can lead to a concrete ethics. The answer is simple. Value in Sartre's definition is so abstract that it readily associates with any concrete set of values. The abstract idealism and monism of the Value on the one hand, and the concrete relativism and pluralism of values on the other, are complementary expressions of dynamic nihilism. Sartre's ethics is concrete only in the sense in which opportunism is concrete. The nature of value, according to him, can be defined in universal terms, but not so values. Each of them exists solely by virtue of my recognizing it as value. "It follows that my freedom is the sole foundation of values and that nothing, absolutely nothing, justifies me in adopting this or that particular value, this or that scale of values. As a being through which values exist, I am unjustifiable. And my freedom is anguished at being the unfounded foundation of values" (p. 76).

How this general thesis can be applied to actual situations becomes fairly clear from Sartre's pamphlet *L'existentialisme est un humanisme* and Simone de Beauvoir's *L'existentialisme et la sagesse des nations* (Paris, 1948). Both these booklets are written *ad usum Delphini*, with a marked desire to make Existentialism appear as respectable, optimistic, and pleasing to the "decent people" as possible. The suggestion made by Marxists that here a new ideology of the Radical Socialist party (France's liberal socialists) is in the making has a degree of plausibility. The articles contributed by the two writers to *Temps Modernes* provide further information.

In the first place the suspicion of reckless libertarianism is removed. The individual's privilege to choose his values in complete freedom and without regard to the authority of traditional values as embodied in the "wisdom of the nations" does not involve irresponsibility, Sartre contends. His exhortation: remember that you are free, should not be understood to mean: do what you please. For the chooser does not choose for himself alone—he chooses for all individuals. In him humanity is embodied. And no repentance, no expiation, no forgiving God (there is no God) can undo what man does. So, a truly superhuman burden of responsibility is heaped upon the agent's shoulders. Furthermore, being free himself, the individual cannot without contradiction violate the freedom of others. Through his being with others, an essential feature of human individuality, his freedom limits itself. It ceases to be absolute freedom.

All this is very noble. At the same time it is easily identified as a quotation from Kant. But in Kant the self-limiting freedom—the principle that no individual should be used as a means towards an end other than himself—rests on the solid foundation of a concept of reason. The will as truly free is for Kant identical with practical reason *in actu.* In Sartre the same principle is a gratuitous affirmation. Not only does it lack the supporting idea of reason, but it contradicts the Existentialist premises. Developed into its consequences it would result, just as it does in Kant, in universal rules of conduct. These rules as enunciated by Kant in the various formulae of the Categorical Imperative are, it is true, very general, and therefore of uncertain applicability to concrete cases. But they have precisely that character which values do not and should not have according to Sartre: they exist independently of our consent. They have a foundation other than our bottomless freedom. Sartre's ethics clearly defines a position not only beyond crisis but beyond Existentialism.

The eclectic character of this pseudo-Existentialist ethics permits the incorporation of Aristotle's idea of the Golden Mean. On the one extreme, Simone de Beauvoir asserts, we find "the serious man" who forgets his freedom over his commitment to a cause or a given set of values. On the other extreme the nihilist, engrossed in his freedom, shrinks from every commitment. The Existentialist strikes the happy medium: he devotes himself to a cause without surrendering to it. While pursuing a concrete goal he aims through that goal at something else—not, however, at another finite and concrete cause but at liberty itself, the "free movement of existence" ("Pour une morale de l'ambiguité," *Les Temps Modernes*, II [14 Nov. 1946], p. 207; cf. also II [15 Dec. 1946], pp. 385–408).

To aim at "the free movement of existence" is still too general a direction for one who tries to take his bearings in the crosscurrents of his time. But the resourceful Sartre knows how to fill this want. The revolutionary act, he affirms, is "the free act *par excellence*" ("Matérialisme et Révolution," *Les Temps Modernes*, I [10 July 1946], p. 26). Revolution, in turn, he identifies with progress, and he recommends Existentialism as the philosophy of revolutionary progress as well as of socialism. The Existentialist hurries to the barricades though he has as yet failed to identify the oppressors. The philosopher turns orator: "Truth itself is revolutionary. Not the abstract truth of idealism but Truth concrete, willed, created, upheld, conquered through social struggles by the men who work for the liberation of man" (*ibid.*, p. 31). Liberalism since its inception has been animated by faith in the dignity of man—a fine and true faith, though, cut from its theological moorings, it may blind the believer to the wickedness of man. For Sartre man is neither good nor wicked —he is Nothing, though a very dynamic Nothing. No wonder that his political pathos sounds hollow. With a strident voice, "liberalism" in agony babbles meaningless slogans: liberty for liberty's sake, emancipation for emancipation's sake, revolution for revolution's sake. Much against his will Sartre shows us how completely European liberalism is at its wit's end. Europe in distress looks towards France, and France makes herself heard indeed. But through the Existentialists she does not speak with the accents of her mellow wisdom.

In the last analysis, Sartre's line of retreat from Existentialism lies parallel to that of Heidegger. If the deification of actual history can be regarded as the core of Hegel's teaching, we find in Sartre the same return from Existentialism to its historical source that is evident in Heidegger's development. Sartre, too, reverts through Kant to Hegel—not to the Hegel inflamed by Hölderlin's historical-eschatological vision but to the Hegel who defined history as the growth of freedom. In both thinkers the Titanism of defiant freedom collapses into subservience to the actual trend of affairs glorified as progress. And both debar themselves from an understanding of history as the testing ground of human freedom. History becomes for them the embodiment of divinity. So, instead of meeting God in history, they mistakenly try to know Him through history, His least transparent veil.

(3) For the Christian the dilemma which forces the other Existentialists out of Existentialism is resolved in the idea of faith. To state the dilemma once more: after a position beyond the crisis is attained, it must be possible to give

a rational explanation of crisis from this position. But crisis, rationally explained, is no longer crisis. Again, if this explanation is not possible, we are confronted with two unrelated and mutually incompatible theories—one that issues in crisis, the other that emerges out of it—which is an absurdity.

Faith, according to Kierkegaard, consists precisely in the acceptance of this absurdity. The believer, he holds, believes by virtue of the absurd. Acceptance of this thesis disposes of the dilemma and, at the same time, of all imaginable dilemmas, so setting an end to debate. By deliberately embracing an absurdity we draw up a death warrant for the intellect and we should from then on keep our peace. Or if further discourse is desired, it should be limited to two purposes: to an exposition of faith on the level of absurdity (a faith intellectually indefensible as well as unassailable) and to exhortatory, biographical-historical accounts of the agony of the intellect.

The negatively or formally absurd is to be distinguished from the positively or materially absurd. Following Sartre we may, for example, consider *The Stranger* by Camus a specimen of the "novel of the absurd" (*cf.* Victor Brombert, "Camus and the Novel of the 'Absurd,'" *Yale French Review*, I [July 1948], 119–23). The indifference to meaning and responsibility in the chief character strikes the reader as a negation of his "normal" insistence on meaning and sense of responsibility and creates the impression of absurdity. A fundamental and, we feel, deeply justified expectation meets no fulfillment in an estranged world. This negative absurdity differs from the positive and, we are tempted to say, aggressive absurdity which is the basis of Kierkegaardian faith. In the story of Abraham and Isaac as interpreted in *Fear and Trembling*, God's command to Abraham is meaningless, not only in the negative sense of "unmeaning," but it runs counter to meaning. It is an affront to the human craving for meaning. More than that, it has the appearance of evil. Abraham is ordered to slaughter his son, and this by itself is an outrage against which both paternal affection and respect for human life cry out in indignation. Then it is his son Isaac who is to be immolated, he who is so visibly God's special and miraculous gift to his parents and the pledge of the great promise made to Abraham by God. And this to all appearances senseless, cruel, wicked, and perfidious order is obeyed by Abraham. By this obedience he proves himself a "hero of faith." For faith, according to Kierkegaard, consists precisely in the inner movement of the absurd by which man subjects himself to God as the wholly other, the terrible majesty of a power revealed to man only in the extinction of human hopes, the crumbling of human systems of philosophy, theology, and morality, and in the downfall of civilizations. Crisis is the burning bush out of which God speaks to man. The absurd seized upon by faith is an affirmative power and a particular absurdity.

In interpreting the Incarnation, the central mystery of Christianity, theologians and mystics have striven to maintain a balance of two aspects. On the one hand, they have pointed out the naturalness of the event by developing its social and cosmic affinities and effects within a sacramental universe. Christ is God's only-begotten Son, coequal with the Father. But in a much humbler sense we too may boast to be God's children and thereby Christ's brothers. Christ is "very God of very God" but He is also the "second Adam," the paragon of that same humanity that was marred by the first Adam. Christ came into the world to save sinners, that is, human beings who are "only a little below the angels." But it is also said, by St. Paul, that not only we but "the whole creation groaneth and travaileth in pain together until now" (Rom. 8:22). On the other hand, the character of the event as a mystery is emphasized. As a mystery it remains ultimately unassimilable to the other facts which compose the universe. It has to be accepted on faith, in spite of the shock which it administers to our sense of the probable and fitting in nature. It is a stumbling block to the legalists in morality, and an offense to rationalist philosophers. Considered as a proposition, faith is absurd. Here the "absurd," a word put in currency by Tertullian, has its proper place and function.

In Kierkegaard this balance of aspects is destroyed. The King of kings born in a stable, God, creator of heaven and earth, wrapped in swaddling clothes and lying in a manger, the Infinite enclosed in human finitude—this is not only above but against all understanding. And precisely this offense to reason is, according to Kierkegaard, the challenge which faith meets. With him the absurd moves into the center and becomes the core of faith. The story of the nativity is divested of its pastoral sweetness, and that faded antique glory which the Evangelists spread around the scion of the house of King David is wiped from the Child's brow. Stark poverty and miserable helplessness are to shock us into an awareness of the great paradox: God became man.

It is necessary once more to call attention to a point which, subtle though it may seem, is of cardinal importance. Philosophy operating with the method of existential analysis can attain only to a negative and general idea of the absurd. By speaking of the "unity of the Infinite and the Finite" (using a shred of Hegelian metaphysics to which he is hardly entitled), Kierkegaard confers no more than the semblance of positivity on that *negativum*, that absence of basic fitness, that Great Incongruity. Faith, however, deals with a specific and positive absurdity. So there is no plausible transition from the experience of the generally and negatively absurd, the crisis, to the seizure by the movement of faith of a particular absurdity. This lack of sequence is recognized by Kierkegaard as a "qualitative leap." The consequences of this rupture in the process of spiritual life are grave. When Karl Barth roused lethargic Protestantism by administering to it a strong dose of the passion of crisis, he, as heir to Kierkegaard, contracted also the debts of his great precursor. He had to put up with the rupture and discontinuity involved in crisis theory. The inconveniences flowing from this element of "leap" prompted him gradually to shift the center of gravity of his teaching from crisis and despair to the position beyond the crisis—the Word of God as received by the faithfully penitent church. Although Barth, as a Christian theologian, has never been fully within the sphere of Existentialism, we notice also in his case the characteristic recoiling from Existentialism. The line of retreat is marked by this writer's development from his revolutionary commentary on the Epistle to the Romans (*Der Römerbrief*, 1918) to the constructive theology of his *Kirchliche Dogmatik* (1932——), the monumental work which is still in process.

Since there is an unaccountable leap from the general absurdity experienced in crisis to the specific absurdity of particular faith, apologetics as a branch of theology has to be lopped off. For apologetics tries to achieve rational plausibility. But reason in its negative use can achieve only the crisis, preparing for the plunge into general absurdity

—it has nothing to suggest regarding the particular absurdity of Christian faith. So rational argument, it appears, can be a preamble to faith only, and not to the Christian faith. Barth, however, abhors the generalities of religious faith and religion as a generic concept. He even rejects the classification of Christianity under monotheism. The God who speaks out of the burning bush is not a Supreme Being, not the God of scholars and philosophers, but the God of Abraham, the God of Isaac, the God of Jacob, he contends. So, according to Barth's own principles, the inducement of crisis through existential analysis is of doubtful value. It may prepare the mind for idolatrous fanaticism as well as for Christian faith. In obviating this criticism Barth distinguishes the crisis in which the Word of God is heard as something totally different from the existential crisis in general. With this emphatic distinction Barth abandons Existentialism as a rational-dialectical procedure. Hand in hand with this surrender goes a change in homiletic approach. Barth, in writing his commentary on the Epistle to the Romans during the first World War, thought it wise to shatter complacency and to create a disturbance in the minds of his contemporaries by telling them of despair and crisis. He does not think so now after another and still more terrible war has devastated our world. Though he still holds that the Word of God can be properly understood only by a spirit broken in crisis, he prefers not to take a hand in producing this prerequisite but rather to speak out of faith in interpreting the Word in and for the church.

Another inconvenience of the principle of discontinuity becomes alarmingly clear as soon as the attempt is made to develop the affirmation of dialectical theology into a dogmatic position, in other words, when the theological appeal is to develop into a theology. Reason is needed to carry out this constructive work. But reason, battered by furious existential criticism, robbed, so to speak, of its honor by the triumph of the absurd, and limited to a creation fashioned by *Eros*, self-assertive love, rather than Godward love, *Agape* (*Römerbrief* [2nd ed.; München, 1922], p. 421)—of what use can this defeated reason be in so great a task? The problem consists in knowing how to speak without contradiction of an abyss in which reason perishes and yet to take reason across the abyss for purposes of dogmatic exegesis and construction. In an attempt to justify the unjustifiable, Barth must assert that the comprehension of faith is totally different from natural understanding. In the *Römerbrief* the author, quoting Luther, speaks of the "dark night of faith" (*die Finsterniss des Glaubens*, p. 354). As builder of doctrine he admits more and more light into that darkness but contends that this is not the common light which generally helps us puzzle over our problems and occasionally solve them.

Barth's difficulties are the well-known difficulties of negative theology, aggravated in his case to the point of absurdity. Negative theology from Pseudo-Dionysius down to contemporary neo-Thomists counterbalances its negations by affirmations and through a dialectical process finally rises to its great Negation-Affirmation—God. Every created thing, subjected to dialectical scrutiny, answers with a negation: "I am not God." But presently it adds: "God made me." God is thus the non-Being of everything, while at the same time everything points to Him as to the source of its being. Nothing of this dialectical balance is preserved in Barth's dialectical theology. Crisis, no longer counterpoised by ascent, reigns supreme, and mediation through a hierarchically ordered world is discarded. So God is the non-Being of all mundane things. To the writer of the *Römerbrief* all things declare as with one voice that they are not God, and only their silence about Him suggests that there is a God. Consequently the things of this world must be explained without reference to God, and God must be spoken of without reference to the world. Analogy of being is anathema and the biblical idea of man as the image of God must be explained away.

All things, for Barth, are silent about God. But in one being, in man, silence is guilt, and his guilty silence is, as it were, silently obstreperous. The relations tying the world to God are attenuated only to strengthen the one relation that links sinful man to God his savior. In man, want itself testifies to God. Mankind lies in suffering, and the clue to its affliction is that "God is God" (p. 348). God is linked to the world only through that dramatic negation of a link which is the crisis suffered by man. Thus God's transcendence is exalted above all comprehension. By the same token it is called in question. For negation also establishes a link between its terms, emphatic negation an excessively strong link.

"God is God," "God Himself," "God alone." With tireless insistence these formulae bring home to us the majesty of the Lord God. But at the same time Barth warns us not to mistake God for a divine thing or an objective (*gegenüberstehende*) ideal entity. He must be experienced in existence and understood "as the inscrutable Divine Relation in which we as men find ourselves" (p. 413). God as a divine relation in which we stand—is there not danger of collapsing God's transcendence into human subjectivity? Is it not necessary to love the world more than Barth does (though not for its own sake, but for its being a similitude of God) in order to love God aright? Does not this desperate submission to God bear too close a resemblance to the encounter with Nothingness?

The term crisis is derived from a Greek verb which means to select (as by straining), to judge or test (κρίνειν). Through crisis man is tested. There is no test without a standard by which to test—no crisis without a criterion. The one philosophically significant crisis is the crisis of criteria. In fact, philosophy is this crisis. But this crisis too requires a criterion, and by destroying it crisis destroys itself. Existentialism is a philosophy of crisis and yet annuls crisis. It testifies to a great truth but only in the way in which Jonah testified to God as he fled from Him across the sea towards Tarshish.